The Secret Life of English-Medium Instruction in Higher Education

This volume explores the inner-workings of English-medium instruction (EMI) in higher education (HE) at two universities. After an introductory chapter that sets the scene and provides essential background, there are four empirically based chapters that draw on data collected from a range of sources at two universities in Catalonia. This includes interviews, audio/video recordings of classes, audio logs produced by both lecturers and students, policy documents, students' written work, and student presentation evaluation rubrics. These chapters examine the following issues: (1) the choice of either English or Catalan as the medium of instruction by students and lecturers; (2) how students display ambivalence towards EMI, as well as a general lack of enthusiasm towards and an ironic distance from 'doing education'; (3) how students resist EMI by contravening its English monolingual norm, using their L1s in the classroom; and finally, (4) how EMI lecturers on occasion act as English language teachers despite their continued claims to the contrary. The book ends with a concluding chapter that draws all of the strands together around key themes.

This book is written for scholars interested in issues surrounding EMI in HE in general, as well as those EMI in HE practitioners who have adopted a reflective approach to their professional practice and wish to know more about the ins and outs of EMI in HE from multiple perspectives. It is a useful resource for MA and PhD students on applied linguistics programmes in which the roles and uses of English in HE worldwide are deemed to be important and worthy of attention. Additionally, this will be relevant to courses or modules focusing on language policy, as well as curriculum issues more broadly and language teaching practice more specifically.

David Block is ICREA Research Professor in Sociolinguistics at the Universitat Pompeu Fabra, Spain.

Sarah Khan is Lecturer in the Faculty of Science and Technology at The University of Vic – Central University of Catalonia, Spain.

Routledge Focus on English-Medium Instruction in Higher Education

Professional Development for EMI faculty in Mexico
The case of Bilingual, International, and Sustainable Universities
Myrna Escalona Sibaja

Supporting EMI students outside of the classroom
Evidence from Japan
Rachael Ruegg

The Secret Life of English-Medium Instruction in Higher Education
Examining Microphenomena in Context
Edited by David Block and Sarah Khan

To access the full list of titles, please visit: https://www.routledge.com/Routledge-Focus-on-English-Medium-Instruction-in-Higher-Education/book-series/RFEHE

The Secret Life of English-Medium Instruction in Higher Education
Examining Microphenomena in Context

Edited by David Block and Sarah Khan

LONDON AND NEW YORK

First published 2021
by Routledge
2 Park Square, Milton Park, Abingdon, Oxon OX14 4RN

and by Routledge
52 Vanderbilt Avenue, New York, NY 10017

First issued in paperback 2022

Routledge is an imprint of the Taylor & Francis Group, an informa business

© 2021 selection and editorial matter, David Block and Sarah Khan; individual chapters, the contributors

The right of David Block and Sarah Khan to be identified as the authors of the editorial material, and of the authors for their individual chapters, has been asserted in accordance with sections 77 and 78 of the Copyright, Designs and Patents Act 1988.

All rights reserved. No part of this book may be reprinted or reproduced or utilised in any form or by any electronic, mechanical, or other means, now known or hereafter invented, including photocopying and recording, or in any information storage or retrieval system, without permission in writing from the publishers.

Trademark notice: Product or corporate names may be trademarks or registered trademarks, and are used only for identification and explanation without intent to infringe.

Publisher's Note
The publisher has gone to great lengths to ensure the quality of this reprint but points out that some imperfections in the original copies may be apparent.

British Library Cataloguing-in-Publication Data
A catalogue record for this book is available from the British Library

Library of Congress Cataloging-in-Publication Data
Names: Block, David, editor. | Khan, Sarah, editor.
Title: The secret life of English-medium instruction in higher education: examining microphenomena in context/edited by David Block and Sarah Khan.
Description: London; New York: Routledge, 2020. | Series: Routledge focus on EMI in higher education | Includes bibliographical references and index. |
Identifiers: LCCN 2020027839 (print) | LCCN 2020027840 (ebook) | ISBN 9780367437725 (hardback) | ISBN 9781003005667 (ebook)
Subjects: LCSH: Native language and education–Spain–Catalonia–Case studies. | English-medium instruction–Spain–Catalonia–Case studies. | English language–Study and teaching (Higher)–Spanish speakers–Case studies.
Classification: LCC LC201.7.S7 S43 2020 (print) | LCC LC201.7.S7 (ebook) | DDC 428.00711–dc23
LC record available at https://lccn.loc.gov/2020027839
LC ebook record available at https://lccn.loc.gov/2020027840

ISBN 13: 978-0-367-61062-3 (pbk)
ISBN 13: 978-0-367-43772-5 (hbk)
ISBN 13: 978-1-003-00566-7 (ebk)

Typeset in Times New Roman
by Deanta Global Publishing Services, Chennai, India

Contents

	List of contributors	vi
	About the book	viii
	Acknowledgments	ix
1	The secret life of English-medium instruction: Setting the scene DAVID BLOCK AND SARAH KHAN	1
2	Language issues in EMI: When lecturers and students can choose the language of instruction ELISABET ARNÓ-MACIÀ AND MARTA AGUILAR-PÉREZ	19
3	'Being a student' and 'doing education': A multimodal analysis of *backstage* and *frontstage* interactional episodes in EMI BALBINA MONCADA-COMAS	43
4	Whispers of resistance to EMI policies: The management of Englishisation through alternative local multilingual practices and dissenting identities MARIA SABATÉ-DALMAU	70
5	NOT English teachers, except when they are: The curious case of oral presentation evaluation rubrics in an EMI-in-HE context DAVID BLOCK AND GUZMAN MANCHO-BARÉS	96
6	The secret life of English-medium instruction unraveled SARAH KHAN	120
	Index	133

Contributors

Marta Aguilar-Pérez is associate professor of English for Specific Purposes at Universitat Politècnica de Catalunya, in Barcelona (Spain). She is interested in academic and disciplinary discourses and in technical and academic communication for foreign language speakers. She has recently published on English-medium Instruction and Internationalization in higher education.

Elisabet Arnó-Macià is associate professor of English for Specific Purposes at Universitat Politècnica de Catalunya at Vilanova i la Geltrú, Barcelona, Spain. Her research interests include English for Specific Purposes, English-medium Instruction and Internationalization in higher education, as well as the role of technology in language education, especially intercultural virtual exchange.

David Block is ICREA research professor in Sociolinguistics at the Universitat Pompeu Fabra, Barcelona, Spain. He has published on a variety of language-related topics, which he examines by drawing on scholarship in Marxist political economy, sociology, and anthropology. Two recent books are *Political economy and sociolinguistics: Neoliberalism, inequality and social class* (2018) and *Post-truth and Political discourse* (2019), and he is currently writing a book on identity in the 21st century.

Sarah Khan is a lecturer in the Faculty of Science and Technology at UVic-UCC, Spain. She is a member of GRAC, the Research Group in Learning and Communication, and is interested in CLIL/EMI, internationalisation, and classroom-based language research. Her work at the UVic-UCC includes teacher training, research, institutional translations, and managing the faculty's international relations.

Guzman Mancho-Barés works in the English and Linguistics Department at the Universitat de Lleida, Spain. He has conducted research on academic and disciplinary communication, internationalization, and multilingualism in higher education, and the impact of EMI on ESP from an academic literacies perspective. In his most recent work, he has focused on EMI lecturers' use of correction as a language teaching resource.

Balbina Moncada-Comas is a PhD student in the English and Linguistics Department at the Universitat de Lleida, Spain. Her research focuses on the study of teachers' and students' identities affected by the implementation of English-medium instruction (EMI). Her research interests include multilingualism and bilingualism, language teaching and learning, CLIL/EMI, identity and language education, and policy in higher education institutions.

Maria Sabaté-Dalmau works in the Departament d'Anglès i Lingüística at the Universitat de Lleida, Spain, where she conducts critical sociolinguistic ethnographic research on multilingual policies and practices, and transnational linguistic identities and ideologies. She is chair of the board of the Catalan Sociolinguistics Society. Her publications include *Migrant Communication Spaces: Regimentation and Resistance* (2014).

About the book

The increase in English-medium instruction (EMI) as part of the general Englishisation of higher education worldwide has generated a great deal of research in recent years. Many aspects of the phenomenon have been put under the microscope, from university language policies to stakeholders' beliefs or attitudes. However, very little research has taken an ethnographically oriented, microscopic view of EMI in action. This edited collection does just this, drawing on data collected over a period of two years in STEM departments at two Catalan universities. The book's editors, David Block and Sara Khan, set the scene in the opening chapter, which is followed by Chapter 2, in which Elisabet Arnó-Macià and Marta Aguilar-Pérez examine why students and the lecturers choose EMI over L1-medium instruction. The remaining chapters describe microphenomena in EMI in action. In Chapter 3, Balbina Moncada-Comas dissects a brief episode of classroom interaction in terms of social identity. In Chapter 4, Maria Sabaté-Dalmau proposes a new critical sociolinguistics 'whispers of resistance' framework for the fine-grained analysis of classroom interaction. In Chapter 5, David Block and Guzman Mancho-Barés explore lecturers' allegiance to their disciplinary identities despite using language criteria when evaluating their students' oral presentations. The book ends with Chapter 6, in which Sarah Khan provides critical commentary on the book's content.

Acknowledgments

We wish to thank the following people for reading and commenting on Chapters 2–5: Emma Dafouz, John Gray, Hartmut Haberland, Francesca Helm, Maria Kuteeva, David Marsh, Ute Smit, Josep Soler Carbonell, and Bob Wilkinson. Their detailed and perceptive comments were essential to making these chapters better. Special thanks go to Alison Stewart who read a final version of the manuscript and made extremely helpful comments on the overall content and coherence of the volume.

We thank the people at Routledge who have guided us through different stages of the shaping of this book – ShengBin Tan, Katie Price, Sarah Silva, and Louisa Semlyen – as well as the editors of the Routledge Focus on English-Medium Instruction in Higher Education series – Annette Bradford and Howard Brown.

We thank the authors of Chapters 2–5 for being punctual and pertinent to the overall aims of the volume, and for being attentive to our requests for different types of information along the way.

We thank the Spanish Ministry of Economy, Industry and Competitiveness (*El Ministerio de Economía, Industria y Competitividad* – MINECO) for granting funding for the research project 'Towards an empirical assessment of the impact of English-medium instruction at university: language learning, disciplinary knowledge and academic identities' (ASSEMID), which produced the data discussed in this volume (Code FFI2016-76383-P; 30 December 2016–29 December 2019).

Finally, although it may sound odd, we thank each other for being supportive and helpful co-editors.

1 The secret life of English-medium instruction
Setting the scene

David Block and Sarah Khan

Introduction

In 2015, the authors of the chapters that make up this short-form book, along with several other colleagues, began meeting to discuss what would become a research project entitled *Towards an empirical assessment of the impact of English-medium instruction at university: language learning, disciplinary knowledge and academic identities* (ASSEMID). The research proposal that emerged from these meetings was positively evaluated by the Spanish Ministry of Economy, Industry and Competitiveness (*El Ministerio de Economía, Industria y Competitividad* – MINECO), and we were granted funding for the three-year period of December 2016 to December 2019.

The chief aim of ASSEMID was to focus on how English-medium instruction (EMI) in STEM (Science, Technology, Engineering, and Mathematics) subjects was carried out at two Catalan universities – the Universitat de Lleida and the Universitat Politècnica de Catalunya. Our interest in this specific topic came from the experience of team members, who had, over the years, done research on English for Specific Purposes (ESP) and more specifically, English for Academic Purposes (EAP), as well as Content and Language Integrated Learning (CLIL). These researchers were poised to add to their repertoires of knowledge of EMI, given that this modality was progressively taking over spaces where the previous three had, at different times in the past, been prominent.

As EMI has emerged in a range of contexts worldwide, so too has there been an exponential increase in the amount of research that aims to explore it in policy, curricular, and practical terms. In this regard, books on EMI appearing over the past several years include Barnard and Hasim (2018); Bradford and Brown (2018); Breeze and Sancho-Guinda (2017); Brenn-White and Faethe (2013); Dafouz and Smit (2020); Dimova; Hultgren and Jensen (2015); Fenton-Smith; Humphries and Walkinshaw (2017); Fortanet-Gómez (2013); Henrikson; Holmen and Kling (2019); Hultgren; Gregersen and Thøgersen (2014); Hyland and Shaw (2016); Jenkins (2013); Jenkins and Mauranen (2019); Macaro (2018); Mukerji and Tripathi (2013); Murata (2018); Nikula; Dafouz; Moore and Smit (2016); Preisler; Fabricius and Klitgård (2011); Ruiz de Zarobe; Sierra and Gallardo del Puerto (2011); Smit and Dafouz (2012); Valcke and Wilkinson (2017); van der Walt (2013); Wächter and Maiworm (2014); and Zhao and Dixon (2017). In addition, there have been numerous special issues in applied linguistics journals over the past several years (e.g. Doiz and Lasagabaster, 2020; Haberland and Mortensen, 2012; Kuteeva, 2011; Pecorari and Malmström, 2018; Smit and Studer, in press), to say nothing of the growing list of specialised journals such as *Journal of English-Medium Instruction*. The series in which this book appears – the Routledge Focus on English-Medium Instruction in Higher Education, edited by Annette Bradford and Howard Brown – is a further indication that EMI has established itself firmly as a key area of research. Finally, the presence of EMI as an important research focus has been in evidence at applied linguistics conferences and, more recently, there has been a clear increase in the number of conferences devoted exclusively to this topic. More locally, we note how in Spain there is a growing number of academic groups devoting time and attention to EMI in HE, producing suggestive results which, it is hoped, will be taken on board by policy makers and stakeholders in the future. This research is reflected in a series of publications (e.g. Doiz and Lasagabaster, 2020; Fortanet-Gómez, 2013; and contributions to collections such as Breeze and Sancho-Guinda, 2017; Doiz et al., 2013; Lasagabaster and Ruiz de Zarobe, 2010; Ruiz de Zarobe et al., 2011). In our research, and in this book more specifically, we align ourselves with these publications and aim to further the discussion and debate about this context and EMI in HE more broadly.

We believe that this short-form collection distinguishes itself from previous publications on EMI, not so much for one single defining characteristic, but for how it combines several characteristics existent elsewhere but that have never before been combined in the way we have combined them here. First, it explores events in a somewhat (though not completely) unique EMI context, in which the dynamic is English in addition to two local languages (Catalan and Spanish), as opposed to English in addition to one local language. Similar contexts exist in other parts of the world: for example, Finnish and Swedish are official languages in Finland, Arabic and Hebrew in Israel, Belarusian and Russian in Belarus, Greek and Turkish in Cyprus, and in Spain itself, Basque and Spanish in the Basque Country. However, as Elliott, Vila and Gilabert (2018, p. 122) suggest: 'Catalonia offers a sociolinguistic situation which is particularly interesting as far as HE language policies are concerned, given its complex sociolinguistic reality and its long history of language contact and language conflict'. This complexity arises from several factors. First, Catalan in HE co-exists with not one but two languages with claims to being international – English *and* Spanish. Second, against some odds, over the past four decades Catalan has experienced a remarkable recovery as regards its use in wide range of social and institutional contexts in Catalonia, to the point that there are perhaps as many as ten million speakers in Spain, France, and Italy. Third and finally, there is the fact that while Catalan has status as an autochthonous language and is the near exclusive official language of education in primary and secondary school, it nonetheless shares considerable space with Spanish at the HE level. These signs of complexity are evidence in the aforementioned trilingual contexts; however, in them the three languages in play are not used or distributed across communicative settings in the same way. Thus, for example, while Hebrew shares space with two international languages (English and Arabic), its sociohistorical recovery post-World War Two was very different from what occurred with Catalan from the late 1970s onwards. In addition, the current language contact dynamics in Israel, involving Hebrew and Arabic, are very different from what one finds in Catalonia, involving Spanish and Catalan. Hebrew can be said to be in a much more powerful position of dominance than Catalan, which shares far more social and institutional space with Spanish. Similarly, while Basque, like Catalan, shares space with Spanish, its relative presence in social and institutional settings is very different from what one finds in Catalonia; it can claim a far lower percentage of daily users than Catalan.

Secondly, the chapters in this volume report on events taking place in a Southern European (SE) context, which is very different from what one finds in Northern, Central, or Eastern European contexts, to say nothing of contexts in East Asia and other Pacific locations. Due to under-resourcing and (unfortunately) a lack of planning, EMI in HE in many parts of Southern Europe is conceived and implemented in very unique ways. EMI began later there than elsewhere in Europe and particular concerns have been whether lecturers and students' English proficiency is sufficient for EMI to be a viable alternative to L1-mediated instruction (Aguilar, 2017; Dafouz, 2018). A disconcerting finding by Costa and Coleman (2010) in Italy was that many Italian lecturers had to teach through EMI regardless of their English language competence and that 77% of institutions that answered a survey claimed that they provided no linguistic or methodological training for lecturers (Costa, 2013). Although some ten years later conditions have no doubt improved in Southern European contexts, the relative gap existent between these contexts and other European contexts remains.

Thirdly, in terms of methodology, this book provides a relatively under-researched approach to EMI with data collected from multiple sources, including questionnaires, interviews, audio and video recordings of classes, audio logs produced by both lecturers and students, policy documents, course materials, exams, students' written work, lecturers' power point slides, and evaluation rubrics, resulting in an ethnographic approach to the study of two EMI in HE contexts. Research on EMI in HE to date has tended to be based on language policy, language curriculum development, teacher education (and especially, teacher cognition), and narrative studies, and most research has drawn on either one data source (e.g. based on questionnaires or interviews) or two data sources (at times combining questionnaires and interviews). Some research that is based on questionnaires and/or interviews also includes the analysis of documents. However, apart from notable exceptions (e.g. Fortanet-Gomez, 2013; Smit, 2010), there is a real paucity of publications in which researchers use the aforementioned data sources in addition to fieldnotes based on the observation of classes; the description, categorisations, and analysis of classroom interaction; and the interpretation and analysis of diaries or logs collected from stakeholders. For example, Dimova, Hultgren and Jensen's (2015) *English-medium instruction in European higher education* contains 14 chapters, with just one (Arkin and Osam, 2015) adopting a truly multi-dimensional approach to data collection in an attempt to view the EMI experience through as many windows as possible. Meanwhile Valcke and Wilkinson's (2017) *Integrating content and language in higher education* does slightly better in this regard, with three out of 13 chapters (Costa and Mariotti, 2017; Gierlinger, 2017; Simbolon, 2017) drawing on multiple data sources. Other edited collections show a similar pattern.

Finally, the ASSEMID project was set up as an attempt to provide a 'warts-and-all' examination of EMI in HE in action, to explore aspects of its implementation that are not always obvious to administrators or even EMI lecturers. In short, it aimed to examine what we are here calling the 'secret life of EMI', understood as the microphenomena that often elude detection. Summed up succinctly, our main argument is that by documenting and analysing minute, fleeting, and often unnoticed occurrences, we can gain a deeper understanding of EMI in HE. Thus while the growth of EMI may be driven top-down, by market forces rather than educational goals (more on this below), a deeper understanding of EMI at the grassroots level is nevertheless essential in making more detailed and research-driven recommendations for both policy and curricular changes to ensure quality learning and teaching practice. We believe – or in any case, it is our hope – that our examination of the secret life of EMI will allow us to hold up a mirror, not only to programme coordinators and administrators who are implementing EMI in HE in less than ideal circumstances in Spain and Catalonia, but also to those working further afield, including in contexts where EMI is being implemented in a more organised and rigorous way.

Setting the scene 5

In the remainder of this introductory chapter, we provide further necessary background information for the remaining five chapters of this volume. First, we discuss the interrelated processes of internationalisation and Englishisation in HE as the general backdrop to the adoption of EMI. We then continue with a definition of the term EMI and how it relates to a more recent coinage, EME (English-medium education), and this is followed by background information about the two research sites focused on in this book – the Universitat de Lleida (UdL) and the Universitat Politècnica de Catalunya (UPC). We end the chapter with a short summary of Chapters 2–5.

Internationalisation and Englishisation

It is now something of a truism to say that HE institutions worldwide have undergone intensive processes of internationalisation over the past several decades (Ennew and Greenaway, 2012; Hultgren et al., 2014; Law and Hoey, 2018). The internationalisation of HE is generally understood to be a response to the marketisation of education, and it dates from the early 1990s, by which time neoliberal economic policies had been applied to just about every economy in the world in one form or another (Block, 2018). Writing about British HE in the early 1990s, Norman Fairclough was prescient in his assessment of what was to come:

> Institutions of higher education come increasingly to operate (under government pressure) as if they were ordinary businesses competing to sell their products to consumers. ...For example, universities are required to raise an increasing portion of their funds from private sources, and increasingly to put in tenders for funding... [I]nstitutions are making major organisational changes which accord with a market mode of operation, such as introducing an 'internal' market by making department more financially autonomous, using 'managerial' approaches, for example, staff appraisal and training, introducing institutional planning, and giving much more attention to marketing. There has been pressure for academics to see students as 'customers'.
>
> (Fairclough, 1993, p. 143)

Fast-forwarding some three decades and we are seeing how Fairclough's predictions are being played out around the world. Thus, universities today are progressively expected to operate as if they were businesses, competing with other businesses in the same sector. As Fairclough noted, there has been a streamlining of bureaucracies and the implementation of measures to control and quantify academic staff performance. Internationalisation also means an increase in the number of alliances and agreements with universities situated around the world, and this leads to a concomitant increase in student and staff mobility in the form of exchange programmes and the active recruitment of students from other countries (international universities actually compete for students as the latter come to be positioned as 'clients', and as Fairclough notes, 'customers'). Internationalisation also means the organisation of events and activities that bring together universities, academics, and students situated in different nation states.

According to authors such as Egron-Polak (2012), internationalisation benefits universities greatly. Among other things, it can enhance academic staff's research capacity, overall knowledge bases, and the quality of teaching. All of this is a result of contacts with scholars from other international universities. Students also benefit from the broadening of horizons that internalisation brings, as study abroad and exchange programmes put them in contact with different cultures and ways of life (both as guests and as hosts). In effect, and due to these improvements in the quality of academic staff and students, internationalised HE institutions are said to gain prestige and status, with greater cultural capital in the local and international university market. Meanwhile, there is a monetary argument in favour of internationalisation: it leads to the generation of more income through internationally and globally funded research projects and a notable increase in tuition fee income, if and where international students pay more than home students.

Authors writing about internationalisation in HE often adopt a relatively uncritical stance towards the process, generally citing positive effects, such as those outlined in the previous paragraph, while ignoring the negative effects of the marketisation of education. Thus, while it might look like a good thing for universities to earn more money, surely the collection of ever-higher tuition fees serves to accelerate the transformation of universities into businesses. In addition, as noted above, in recent years we have seen ever greater controls on academic staff activity, which means that the positive effects of internationalisation cited above are mitigated by the fact that the gains to academic staff are factored into accountability regimes and therefore come to be part of systems to control academics rather than liberate them. Finally, the cosmopolitism that comes with student mobility has also been co-opted by neoliberal rationalities (Dardot and Laval, 2013), such that the knowledges and dispositions acquired from these experiences are now mainly seen as part of the contemporary student's skillset (Flores, 2013; Kubota, 2016; Urciuoli, 2008). In short, internationalised HE institutions are, ultimately, highly complicit with the spread and imposition of neoliberal values and practices (Collini, 2012, 2018; Smyth, 2017; Williams, 2013).

Independently of whether we see internationalisation of HE as strictly positive, or as strictly negative, or as something in between, there is little doubt that outside English-speaking countries an increasingly important pillar in the process has been *Englishisation*. Englishisation may be defined as the use of English in contexts where previously local languages were used. As is the case with internationalisation in HE, Englishisation may be seen as a fairly benign process, something which *just is*, because the world is evolving in the way that it is. Even if we may have *some* reservations about allowing English in as the medium of activity in a growing number of domains, there is evidence in many contexts of a more resigned general sense of TINA (there is no alternative) – the genie has too long been out of the bottle to be put back in, so it is a question of making our way in an increasingly Englishised world as we attempt to maintain as much of local language and culture as possible.

This is the angle on Englishisation that we see in STEM contexts such as the ones examined in this book. For example, when asked about the Englishisation of HE and activities such as EMI which are part of it, Carles, an EMI coordinator in the engineering department at the UdL, had the following to say:

> for the future we need to evolve/if I said before that engineers because of their professional environment need and will need English/because the market is large and you can make it here and sell in China or Australia or wherever/as a university we have to do the same/because if not/really what we will end up being is a local university.
> (CS, 16 January 2018)[1]

In this short response, Carles seems to follow Fairclough's (op. cit.) assessment of British HE in the early 1990s without question: the international HE market and the professional environment of engineers dictate that English is necessary and ignoring these realities means being 'local', that is, marginal and insignificant. However, as we see in Fairclough's early critique, and indeed the critiques of other authors such as Robert Phillipson (1992) and Alastair Pennycook (1994), focusing specifically on the global spread of English and published at more or less the same time, Carles presents a view here that has for some time now been challenged as overly complacent, if not celebratory of Englishisation processes. For Phillipson (2009), one of the dangers presented by the spread of English in HE is *domain loss*, which is what occurs when progressively more and more activities intrinsic to academia, or associated with it, are carried out in English, and not local languages. Thus, for some time now, there has been a trend in academic publishing to value articles, books chapters, and monographs written in English over those produced in other languages. In addition, conferences with names bearing the adjective 'international' have progressively become near or complete English-only zones. Indeed, international conference organisers and participants all too often appear to be oblivious to the gross inherent contradiction at work here. While there is much debate over whether or not domain loss actually exists, or occurs, for example, when English becomes the primary medium of activities in HE (Ferguson, 2006; Haberland, 2005, 2019; Hultgren, 2018), we still might prefer to think that the construct has some use. There is always the common-sense argument that if a language is not used in a particular domain, it will over time, atrophy and become inappropriate and/or inadequate for activities and practices taking place in that domain. However, it is perhaps best to consider domain loss not as an obvious and all-or-nothing process but as one which is gradual as well as partial.

More specifically, Englishisation means that administrative staff are expected to be able to use English as a *lingua franca* in order to attend to the increasing number of international students who have come as a result of the aforementioned international recruitment and exchange policies (more on this below). In many such contexts, this aspect of Englishisation is very much a work in progress as staff are not always prepared to cover all aspects of their work in English. In addition, there are university webpages, and indeed all information produced for public consumption by universities. This information is usually provided bilingually (in official monolingual contexts, the addition of English makes that context bilingual) and multilingually (in officially bilingual and multilingual contexts, English is the privileged additional language). However, once again, the outcomes of Englishisation can be patchy, as webpages often do not make vital information for students available in English or, what is perhaps worse, the information provided in English is not often clearly presented (and may even be incorrect!). Finally, Englishisation means that a part of the curriculum on offer in different subject areas is planned, delivered, and assessed in English, which is our concern in this book.

EMI and EME

In the introduction of this chapter, we mentioned a shortlist of key terms and their acronyms – ESP, EAP, CLIL and EMI. As the most recent educational option to combine English and content teaching, EMI is very different from the previously cited modalities. At the beginning of a research report on EMI worldwide, Julie Dearden offers the following definition of EMI: 'The use of the English language to teach academic subjects (other than English itself) in countries or jurisdictions where the first language (L1) of the majority of the population is not English' (Dearden, 2015, p.

2). This definition is of some use, but it ultimately raises more questions than it answers, not least the entire matter of how the 'countries and jurisdictions' mentioned generate and shape very different types of EMI. In an attempt to fill this informational gap, Will Baker and Julia Hüttner (2017) have suggested that there are, broadly speaking, three general types of EMI programme.

The first type of programme is what Baker and Hüttner call 'student-mobility programmes', by which they mean programmes in non-Anglophone contexts attracting students from a range of countries around the world. These students either are or become, by default, English as a *lingua franca* (ELF) users, as English becomes the language of both their social and academic activities. It should be noted that the Erasmus programme, the student mobility programme *par excellence*, was not set up in 1987 with the goal of prompting the use of ELF; rather it envisioned young Europeans learning the full range of the official languages in the European area where it is in operation. Indeed, to this day, there is nowhere in the statutes or official discourses of the Erasmus programme any reference to the need or desirability for young Europeans to communicate with one another in English. Nevertheless, on the ground, and as understood by those who elaborate the internationalisation policies of universities in the European Higher Education Area (EHEA), English dominates as the *lingua franca*. This is equally, if not more, the case in other HE contexts around the world where student mobility programmes exist. In addition, where HE has adopted more business-like models with regard to the costing of their operations (e.g. the UK, Switzerland), and especially in contexts where students from abroad pay higher tuition fees, student mobility programmes become lucrative businesses.

The second type of EMI programme proposed by Baker and Hüttner is 'internationalization at home programmes', a term used some years ago by Bengt Nilsson (2003; see also Dafouz, 2014). Writing about Swedish universities, but with obvious resonances to other contexts, Nilsson put forth the view that in any higher education internationalisation process: 'the university cannot restrict itself to the mobility of some percentage of students and staff' and that because '[i]t is impossible to send out all students and staff on international exchange..., much work must be done at home' (Nilsson, 2003, p. 34). In internationalisation at home contexts, there is the incorporation of intercultural perspectives; the inclusion of content that addresses global issues and not just local ones; participation in activities that reach out to HE institutions in other countries, (e.g. joining international organisations and consortia); and participation in activities which are intrinsically international in nature (e.g. the organisation of international conferences).

The third type of programme discussed by Baker and Hüttner is 'Anglophone-context programmes'. These programmes are situated in contexts in which English is the dominant language and they therefore are not EMI programmes in the strictest sense of the term, if we follow Dearden's definition cited previously. However, over the past six decades there has been a massive internationalisation and *multilingualisation* of student bodies in countries such as the United States, Canada, the UK, Australia, and New Zealand, which has occurred due to a general increase in migration worldwide and most importantly, because HE in these countries has become more entrepreneurial as universities have actively sought out overseas students who pay higher tuition fees. Relevant here is how university programmes in these settings have come to take on some of the characteristics of EMI programmes elsewhere in the world. This is especially the case linguistically, as a critical mass of international students will often mean the emergence of an ELF environment which shares characteristics with the linguistic environments that emerge in EMI programmes outside the Anglophone world.

The chapters in this book are based on two HE contexts which to varying degrees fall somewhere between Baker and Hüttner's 'student-mobility' and 'internationalisation at home' programmes. We say this because both the UPC and the UdL both apparently *intend* to be in the former category, as they express an interest in internationalisation and a diverse student body in their official discourses. However, neither university achieves this goal to a significant degree, although the UPC has a higher international profile than the UdL. Indeed, in the latter setting, we found EMI courses with no international students at all and many with only a small number (under 5%). In this sense, the contexts examined in this book are more in the realm of constructing internationalisation at home than importing it from abroad.

Apart from a consideration of EMI typologies, it is also necessary to address three additional factors introduced by Emma Dafouz and Ute Smit (2016, 2020) in their recent work. First, there is the matter of how EMI contexts do not just involve the 'instruction' represented by the letter 'I' in the acronym; rather they include a broad range of curricular activities that may be said to constitute education. These range from the establishment of what content is to be taught in English to how students will be assessed in English. Given this situation, Dafouz and Smit suggest it is more appropriate to call the object of study here EME (English-medium education) and not EMI. Nevertheless, in this book we adopt the acronym EMI as we believe it captures more accurately the range of phenomena explored in the four main content chapters, which are all in the realm of teaching (i.e. instruction).

Setting the scene 11

Two additional factors addressed by Dafouz and Smit are EME contexts as multidimensional and multiscalar in nature (indeed, like most social phenomena) and how this complexity increases considerably when it occurs in multilingual settings. In an attempt to capture this multi-levelled reality, Dafouz and Smit (2016, 2020) have developed an ecological model for the study of 'English-medium education in multilingual university settings' (EMEMUS), situating their research in what has become mainstream 21st century sociolinguistics, based on the foundational work of scholars such as Jan Blommaert (2010) and his 'sociolinguistics of globalization'. Dafouz and Smit propose what they call the 'ROADMAPPING framework', which focuses on six interrelated components in any given EMI context. In somewhat embellished form, these six components (and how they relate to the acronym) look as follows:

1) the roles of English in relation to other languages, which can be complex where English is entering an already crowded linguistic market (RO);
2) academic disciplines, both as broadly defined by international communities of scholars and in more localised varieties (AD);
3) management of the EMI curriculum, which means both language and content management (M);
4) the different agents and/or stakeholders involved (A);
5) the practices and processes constituting EMI (PP);
6) and broader, shaping and structuring discourse, practices and processes such as globalizing forces and flows and the more specific internationalisation of higher education (ING).

(based on Dafouz and Smit, 2016)

The upshot to EMEMUS, as elaborated by Dafouz and Smit, is that, in contexts in which HE has been Englishised, and specifically where EMI has been introduced, there is the need to bear in mind and take on board the complexities that come with such change. The chapters comprising this volume deal with all six of the areas identified by Dafouz and Smit, albeit to varying degrees. This is the case not least because each micro situation that is examined here is necessarily imbedded in and involves: the roles of English in relation to other languages and academic disciplines as communities of practice (Hyland, 2012); EMI as the management of language and disciplinary content; the viewpoints and activities of different agents and stakeholders; practices and processes as constitutive of EMI as an emergent phenomenon; and finally, broader globalising and internationalising discourses that shape and structure EMI.

12 *David Block and Sarah Khan*

EMI at the Universitat de Lleida and Universitat Politècnica de Catalunya

Catalonia has 12 universities, eight of which are found in or around Barcelona. According to the CIC (Inter-university Council of Catalonia), English and other third languages have been promoted since 2014 to improve internationalisation, integration into the EHEA, and employability (CTLU, 2019, p. 3). The CIC has put into practice its aim to 'improve knowledge of a third language, preferably English' for research, teaching, and management at Catalan universities and the number of courses given in a third language (mainly English) has risen accordingly at degree level by 2.5% in 2010 to 11.3% in 2017. A recent law, *Llei 1/2018* (DOGC, 9/5/2018), which was passed with these aims in mind, means that undergraduates need to have a B2 level on the Common European Framework of Reference for Languages (CEFR) in a third language (English, German, French, Italian) by the time they finish their degree. Average figures for 2017 show that 20.4% of master's programmes and 10% of undergraduate programmes at Catalan universities are in 'a third language' (GDLP, 2017 p. 35), with more master's programmes doing so because of the greater number of full-time international students and lecturers on them. Table 1.1 provides some basic figures on the UdL and the UPC, both public universities.

Situated in the west of Catalonia, in Lleida, the UdL has nearly 14,000 students and was founded in 1991. On the other hand, the UPC is one of the universities in the centre of Barcelona, founded in 1971 with over 30,000 students. At both universities the incidence of EMI has increased dramatically. Although EMI has officially been recognised since 2004 in UdL and 2008 in UPC, as part of the universities' internationalisation plans, sources at both universities claim that courses were being taught in English as far back as the 90's or even earlier (Marta Aguilar at UPC; Paquita Santiveri

Table 1.1 Universitat de Lleida and Universitat Politècnica de Catalunya in figures (2016-2017).

	Universitat de Lleida	*Universitat Politècnica de Catalunya*
Location	Lleida	Barcelona
Founding year	1991	1971
Number of students (approx.)	14,000	30,000
Official languages	Spanish, Catalan	Spanish, Catalan
EMI begins	2004	2008
EMI courses	6.1%	17.6%
Full EMI programmes	2 MA	3 undergraduate, 24 MAs

at UdL, personal communication). Data was collected for the ASSEMID project during the 2017–2018 academic year and figures for that year show that 6.1% of all courses were taught in English at UdL and 17.6% at UPC. Most EMI courses are part of the L1-medium undergraduate programmes apart from two MA programmes at UdL and three undergraduate and 24 MA programmes at UPC which are taught entirely in English

This volume

This book is composed of six chapters. In this, the introductory chapter, we have attempted to set the scene for the remainder of the book, providing some key background information.

In Chapter 2, Elisabet Arnó and Marta Aguilar focus on an engineering course at the UPC entitled 'Advanced Electronics', which is offered, simultaneously, in both Catalan and English. In a situation in which both a lecturer and students can choose the language of instruction, their interest is in the reasons provided by participants for choosing one option or the other. Moving from their previous research comparing issues such as class delivery in both languages and participants' views on teaching quality (Aguilar and Arnó, 2020), the authors here draw on questionnaire and interview data in their examination and analysis of how participants experience the course, more general aspects such as how language mediates disciplinary knowledge and finally, the more practical matter of how EMI is implemented.

In Chapter 3, Balbina Moncada-Comas uses multimodal analysis and draws on Erving Goffman's classic work on *backstage* and *frontstage* interaction (Goffman, 1959) as she examines and analyses a videotaped interaction between two students and a lecturer in an EMI engineering class at the UdL. She first documents two students' *backstage* interactions with each other and their *frontstage* interactions with their lecturer. She then contrasts these back and frontstage behaviours, focusing on how students adopt different subject positions depending on whether they are 'being a student' or 'doing education' (Benwell and Stokoe, 2002).

In Chapter 4, Maria Sabaté-Dalmau also adopts a Goffmanian perspective (Goffman, 1959) in which, once again, *frontstage* and *backstage* are key constructs. However, in this case this perspective is embedded in a broader critical sociolinguistics (Heller, 2011) framework and an interest in how larger political economic forces underlie EMI practice at the micro level of classroom interaction. Sabaté-Dalmau documents how a lecturer and her students in a biotechnology course at the UdL both comply with and resist dominant normativities: there is a *frontstage* compliance with disciplinary content transmission via English-only instruction and the adoption of English-user academic identities, which contrasts with *backstage* breaches of the English monolingual norm, what she calls 'whispers of resistance', as agents subvert this norm by interacting in Spanish and Catalan.

In Chapter 5, David Block and Guzman Mancho-Barés are interested in the extent to which two STEM lecturers at the UdL, one an agronomy engineer and the other an infrastructures engineer, contradict the pervasive 'I am not an English teacher' self-positioning that is common across a range of EMI contexts (Airey, 2012; Block and Moncada-Comas, 2019). In order to explore this issue, the authors focus on the specific case of rubrics used to evaluate students' oral presentations given on the last day of courses taught by the two lecturers, as they examine and analyse, in order, the rubrics employed by these lecturers, the lecturers' explanations of the origin and content of the rubrics and finally, how the lecturers provide feedback to their students when the latter give their oral presentations in class.

Finally, in Chapter 6, Sarah Khan brings together the content of Chapters 2–5, drawing out underlying themes and challenges that emerged and discussing: (1) how the different accounts of the secret life of EMI in HE in a single context uncover previously overlooked information for curricular and methodological recommendations in that context, and (2) how these accounts are also relevant to EMI in HE around the world.

Note

1 This excerpt has been translated by David Block from the original in Catalan, which looks as follows:

> 'pel futur necessitem evolucionar/si abans te deia que els enginyers pel seu entorn professional necessiten i necessitaran el anglès/perquè el mercat és gran i tu pots fabricar aquí i vendre a la Xina o a Austràlia o a on sigui/com a universitat hem de fer el mateix/perquè si no/realment el que acabarem sent és una universitat local/' (CS, 16 January 2018).

References

Aguilar, M. (2017). Engineering lecturers' views on CLIL and EMI. *International Journal of Bilingual Education and Bilingualism*, *20*(6), 722–735.

Aguilar, M., & Arnó, E. (2020). 'He's a good lecturer in any language': Shifting from L1 to English and implications for EMI training. In M. Mar Sánchez-Pérez (Ed.), *Teacher training for English medium instruction in higher education* (pp. 153–178). Hershey, PA: IGI-Global.

Airey, J. (2012). "I don't teach language": The linguistic attitudes of physics lecturers in Sweden. *AILA Review*, *25*, 64–79.

Arkin, E., & Osam, N. (2015). English-medium higher education: A case study in a Turkish university context. In S. Dimova, A. K. Hultgren & C. Jensen (Eds.),

English-medium instruction in European higher education (pp. 177–200). Bern: Peter Lang Publishing.
Baker, W., & Hüttner, J. (2017). English and more: A multisite study of roles and conceptualisations of language in English medium multilingual universities from Europe to Asia. *Journal of Multilingual and Multicultural Development, 38*(6), 501–516.
Barnard, R., & Hasim, Z. (Eds.). (2018). *English medium instruction programmes: Perspectives from South East Asian universities*. London: Routledge.
Benwell, B. M., & Stokoe, E. M. (2002). Constructing discussion tasks in university tutorials: Shifting dynamics and identities. *Discourse Studies, 4*(4), 429–453.
Block, D. (2018). *Political economy in sociolinguistics: Neoliberalism, inequality and social class*. London: Bloomsbury Publishing.
Block, D., & Moncada-Comas, B. (2019). English-medium instruction in higher education and the ELT Gaze: STEM lecturers' self-positioning as NOT English language teachers. *International Journal of Bilingual Education and Bilingualism.* doi:10.1080/13670050.2019.1689917.
Blommaert, J. (2010). *The sociolinguistics of globalization*. Cambridge: Cambridge University Press.
Bradford, A., & Brown, H. (Eds.). (2018). *English-medium Instruction at universities in Japan: Policy, Challenges and Outcomes*. Bristol: Multilingual Matters.
Breeze, R., & Sancho-Guinda, C. (Eds.). (2017). *Essential competencies for English-medium university teaching*. Bern: Springer.
Brenn-White, M., & Faethe, E. (2013). *English-taught Master's programs in Europe: A 2013 update*. New York, NY: Institute of International Education.
Collini, S. (2012). *What are universities for?* London: Penguin Books.
Collini, S. (2018). *Speaking of universities*. London: Verso.
Costa, F. (2013). Dealing with the Language Aspect? Personally, no. Content lecturers' views of teaching through English in an ICLHE context. In S. Breidbach & B. Viebrock (Eds.), *CLIL in Europe: Research Perspectives on policy and practice* (pp. 117–127). Bern: Peter Lang Publishing.
Costa, F., & Coleman, J. (2010). Integrating content and language in higher education in Italy: Ongoing research. *International CLIL Research Journal, 1*(3), 19–29.
Costa, F., & Mariotti, C. (2017). Differences in content presentation and learning outcomes in English-medium instruction (EMI) vs. Italian-medium instruction (IMI) contexts. In J. Valcke & R. Wilkinson (Eds.), *Integrating content and language in higher education* (pp. 187–204). Bern: Peter Lang Publishing.
CTLU. (2019). *Informe en compliment de la Resolució 531/XII del Parlament de Catalunya, sobre el nivell de coneixement de terceres llengües a la universitat*. Barcelona: Parlament de Catalunya.
Dafouz, E. (2014). Integrating content and language in European higher education: An overview of recurrent research concerns and pending issues. In A. Psaltov-Joycey, E. Agathopoulou & M. Mattheadakis (Eds.), *Cross-curricular approaches to language education* (pp. 289–304). Cambridge: Cambridge Scholars.
Dafouz, E. (2018). English-medium instruction in multilingual university settings: An opportunity for developing language awareness. In P. Garret & J. M. Cots (Eds.), *The Routledge handbook of language awareness*. London: Routledge.

Dafouz, E., & Smit, U. (2016). Towards a dynamic conceptual framework for English-medium education in multilingual university settings. *Applied Linguistics*, *37*(3), 397–415.

Dafouz, E., & Smit, U. (2020). *ROAD-MAPPING English medium education in the internationalised university*. London: Palgrave Macmillan.

Dardot, P., & Laval, C. (2013). *The new way of the world: On a neoliberal society*. London: Verso.

Dearden, J. (2015). *English as a medium of instruction: A growing global phenomenon*. London: The British Council.

Dimova, S., Hultgren, A. K., & Jensen, C. (Eds.). (2015). *English-medium instruction in European higher education*. Berlin: De Gruyter Mouton.

Doiz, A., & Lasagabaster, D. (Eds.). (2020). The role of languages in English-Medium Instruction (EMI) at university. Special issue of *International Journal of Bilingual Education and Bilingualism*, *23*(3), 257–346.

Doiz, A., Lasagabaster, D., & Sierra, J. M. (Eds.). (2013). *English-medium instruction at universities: Global challenges*. Bristol: Multilingual Matters.

Egron-Polak, E. (2012). Internationalization of higher education: a few global trends and regional perspectives. In C. T. Ennew & D. Greenaway (Eds.), *The globalization of higher education* (pp. 57–69). London: Palgrave Macmillan.

Elliott, N., Vila, F. X., & Gilabert, R. (2018). The presentation of Catalan universities' linguistic reality to a transnational audience. *European Journal of Language Policy*, *10*(1), 121–146.

Ennew, C., & Greenaway, D. (Eds.). (2012). *The globalization of higher education*. London: Palgrave Macmillan.

Fairclough, N. (1993). Critical discourse analysis and the marketization of public discourse: The universities. *Discourse and Society*, *4*(2), 133–168.

Fenton-Smith, B., Humphries, P., & Walkinshaw, I. (Eds.). (2017). *English-medium instruction in higher education in Asia-Pacific: From policy to pedagogy*. Bern: Springer.

Ferguson, G. (2006). *Language planning and education*. Edinburgh: Edinburgh University Press.

Flores, N. (2013). The unexamined relationship between neoliberalism and plurilingualism: A cautionary tale. *TESOL Quarterly*, *47*(3), 500–520.

Fortanet-Gómez, I. (2013). *CLIL in higher education: Towards a multilingual language policy*. Bristol: Multilingual Matters.

GDLP. (2017). *Informe de política lingüística 2017*. Barcelona: Departament de Cultura, Generalitat de Catalunya. Retrieved September 20, 2019, from https://llengua.gencat.cat/web/.content/documents/informepl/arxius/IPL-2017.pdf.

Gierlinger, E. M. (2017). I feel traumatized: Teachers' beliefs on the roles of languages and learning in CLIL. In J. Valcke & R. Wilkinson (Eds.), *Integrating content and language in higher education: Perspectives on professional practice* (pp. 97–116). Bern: Peter Lang.

Goffman, E. (1959). *The presentation of self in everyday life*. London: Penguin.

Haberland, H. (2005). Domains and domain loss. In B. Preisler, A. Fabricus, H. Haberland, S. Kjærbeck, & Risager, K. (Eds.), *The Consequences of mobility: Linguistic and sociocultural contact zones* (pp. 227–237). Roskilde Universitet.

Haberland, H. (2019). Domains. In J. Darquennes, J. C. Salmons & W. Vandenbussche (Eds.), *Language contact: An international handbook* (Vol. 1, pp. 397–405). Berlin: De Gruyter Mouton.

Haberland, H., & Mortensen, J. (Eds.). (2012). Language and the international university. Special issue of *International Journal of the Sociology of Language*, *216*, 1–204.

Heller, M. (2011). *Paths to postnationalism*. Oxford: Oxford University Press

Henrikson, B., Holmen, A., & Kling, J. (2019). *English medium instruction in multilingual and multicultural universities: Academics' voices from the northern European context*. London: Routledge.

Hultgren, A. K. (2018). The Englishization of Nordic universities: What do scientists think? *European Journal of Language Policy*, *10*(1), 77–94.

Hultgren, A. K., Gregersen, F., & Thøgersen, J. (Eds.). (2014). *English in Nordic universities: Ideologies and practices*. Amsterdam: John Benjamins.

Hyland, K. (2012). *Disciplinary identities: Individuality and community in academic discourse*. Oxford: Oxford University Press.

Hyland, K., & Shaw, P. H. (Eds.). (2016). *The Routledge handbook of English for academic purposes*. London: Routledge.

Jenkins, J. (2013). *English as a lingua franca in the international university: The politics of academic English language policy*. London: Routledge.

Jenkins, J., & Mauranen, A. (Eds.). (2019). *Linguistic diversity on the EMI campus: Insider accounts of the use of English and other languages in universities within Asia, Australasia, and Europe*. London: Routledge.

Kubota, R. (2016). Neoliberal paradoxes of language learning: Xenophobia and international communication. *Journal of Multilingual and Multicultural Development*, *37*(5), 467–480.

Kuteeva, M. (Ed.). (2011). Academic English in parallel-language and ELF settings. Special issue of *Ibérica: Journal of the European Association of Languages for Specific Purposes*, *22*, 5–197.

Lasagabaster, D., & Ruiz de Zarobe, Y. (Eds.). (2010). *CLIL in Spain: Implementation, results and teacher training*. Newcastle upon Tyne: Cambridge Scholars Publishers.

Law, D., & Hoey, M. (Eds.). (2018). *Perspectives on the internationalisation of higher education*. London: Routledge.

Macaro, E. (2018). *English-medium instruction*. Oxford: Oxford University Press.

Mukerji, S., & Tripathi, P. (Eds.). (2013). *Handbook of research on transnational higher education*. Hershey, PA: IGI Global Publishers.

Murata, K. (Ed.). (2018). *English-medium instruction from an English as a lingua franca perspective: Exploring the higher education context*. London: Routledge.

Nikula, T., Dafouz, E., Moore, P., & Smit, U. (Eds.). (2016). *Conceptualising integration in CLIL and multilingual education*. Bristol: Multilingual Matters.

Nilsson, B. (2003). Internationalisation at home from a Swedish perspective: The case of Malmö. *Journal of Studies in International Education*, *7*(1), 22–40.

Pecorari, D., & Malmström, H. (Eds.). (2018). At the crossroads of TESOL and English medium instruction. Special issue of *TESOL Quarterly*, *52*(3), 497–720.

Pennycook, A. (1994). *The cultural politics of English as an international language.* London: Longman.
Phillipson, R. (1992). *Linguistic imperialism.* Oxford: Oxford University Press.
Phillipson, R. (2009). *Linguistic imperialism continued.* London: Routledge.
Preisler, B., Fabricius, A., & Klitgård, I. (Eds.). (2011). *Language and learning in the international university: From English uniformity to diversity and hybridity.* Bristol: Multilingual Matters.
Ruiz de Zarobe, Y., Sierra, J. M., & Gallardo del Puerto, F. (Eds.). (2011). *Content and foreign language integrated learning: Contributions to multilingualism in European contexts.* Bern: Peter Lang Publishing.
Simbolon, N. E. (2017). Partial English instruction in English-medium instruction (EMI) practice: Perspectives from lecturers in a university in Indonesia. In J. Valcke & R. Wilkinson (Eds.), *Integrating content and language in higher education* (pp. 167–185). Bern: Peter Lang Publishing.
Smit, U. (2010). *English as a lingua franca in higher education. A longitudinal study of classroom discourse.* Berlin: De Gruyter Mouton.
Smit, U., & Dafouz, E. (Eds.). (2012). Integrating content and language in higher education. *AILA Review, 25,* 1–103.
Smit, U., & Studer, P. (Eds.). (in press). Internationalisation and English medium education: Language, policy and practice. Special issue of *European Journal of Language Policy.*
Smyth, J. (2017). *The toxic university: Zombie leadership, academic rock stars and neoliberal ideology.* London: Palgrave Macmillan.
Urciuoli, B. (2008). Skills and selves in the new workplace. *American Ethnologist, 35*(2), 211–228.
Valcke, J., & Wilkinson, R. (Eds.). (2017). *Integrating content and language in higher education: Perspectives on professional practice.* Bern: Peter Lang.
van der Walt, C. (2013). *Multilingual higher education. Beyond English medium orientations.* Bristol: Multilingual Matters.
Wachter, B., & Maiworm, F. (Eds.). (2014). *English-taught programmes in European higher education: The state of play in 2014.* Bonn: Lemmens Medien GmbH.
Williams, J. (2013). *Consuming higher education: Why learning can't be bought.* London: Bloomsbury Publishing.
Zhao, J., & Dixon, L. Q. (Eds.). (2017). *English-medium instruction in Chinese universities: Perspectives, discourse and evaluation.* London: Routledge.

2 Language issues in EMI

When lecturers and students can choose the language of instruction[1]

Elisabet Arnó-Macià and
Marta Aguilar-Pérez

Introduction

In the context of the ASSEMID research project, the authors of this chapter, from *Universitat Politècnica de Catalunya* (UPC), discovered a scenario that was worth investigating – a lecturer who taught the same electronics course in parallel in Catalan and English. This situation in which the lecturer and the students could choose the language of instruction led us to develop different comparative studies, such as class delivery in both languages and participants' views on teaching quality (Aguilar and Arnó, 2020). Related to *the secret life of EMI*, the title of this book, we were especially interested in unveiling the reasons why participants chose the L1 or the English-medium instruction (EMI) class, in particular when we saw the number of students enrolled in each one (the L1 class outnumbering the EMI one). Our objective was to delve into the reasons (stated or unstated) that lay behind the choice of the language of instruction, analysing a number of issues, from participants' reactions to the course, to more general aspects related to the role of language in the mediation of advanced disciplinary knowledge, and practical questions of EMI implementation.

Context

This study is set at one of several engineering schools at UPC, in Barcelona (Spain), where local students are already bilingual (Catalan and Spanish) and where EMI implementation involves going from bilingualism to multilingualism. University policies promote multilingualism so that lecturers can choose the language of instruction from three options, Catalan, Spanish, and English, and indicate the language in the course documents given to students before enrolment.

The courses taught in English in the school can be summarised as follows: five English for Specific Purposes (ESP) courses and 19 EMI courses, most of them electives. Seven full EMI master's programmes are offered (out of a total of two bachelor's and 13 master's degrees). ESP courses are only offered as electives at bachelor's level. They form part of a common 'bank' of courses, all others being specific to engineering. ESP courses do not have any specific recognition nor are they recommended as preparation for EMI. In practice, this implies that only a small percentage of students follow an ESP course.

This chapter focuses on the master's course *Advanced Electronics*, with parallel EMI (s=15) and L1 (s=71) classes delivered by the same lecturer during the fall semester of 2017. There were no international students in either class and the course was part of a master's programme that grants an engineering license, so it is one of the most popular programmes for domestic students. The *Advanced Electronics* course is mandatory, with approximately 300 students enrolled, who could freely choose among five course group options, depending on the teacher, schedule, or language of instruction. It was departmentally decided that exactly the same materials (in English) and exam would be used for *all* the groups. Exams, however, could be done in any of the three languages. In this particular course, all classes were composed of domestic students; therefore, in this case, the driver for EMI is exposing local students to disciplinary communication in English, rather than facilitating the induction of foreign students.

Literature review

Uncovering realities regarding institutional policies as well as participants' proficiency, attitudes and motivations can yield rich information about the intricacies of EMI. Thus, this chapter draws on two main research strands: implications of the shift from L1 teaching to EMI and participants' motivations and reactions toward EMI when participants can choose the language of instruction.

The first strand refers to the linguistic and methodological difficulties that lecturers and students face in EMI (Ball and Lindsay 2013; Jiang, Zhang and May, 2019; Tsou and Kao, 2017). Studies on language needs point to speaking fluency (Ackerley, 2017) and lack of spontaneity (Guarda and Helm, 2017a; Macaro, Curle, Pun, An and Dearden, 2018). Controversy remains over EMI lecturers' role in developing students' English skills, even if they refuse any accountability on this matter (Airey 2012; Jiang et al., 2019). Lecturers seem to be aware of their lack of oral fluency – especially in general vocabulary and idiomatic expressions, rather than specialised terminology (Ackerley, 2017; Clark, 2017; Dimova and Kling, 2018; Pecorari, Shaw, Irvine and Malmström, 2011). With some exceptions (Guarda and Helm, 2017b), EMI lecturers seem to resort to their L1 teaching approach, relying on their disciplinary expertise and overlooking the impact created by language shift. This is probably due to the assumption that language and disciplinary knowledge can be separated, an epistemological divide that has been questioned (Airey, 2012). Likewise, lecturers' self-reported benefits include increased confidence in their English communication skills, which in turn bolster their mobility and international scientific activity (Aguilar, 2012; Dearden and Macaro, 2016) and appreciation of a more interactive, student-centred pedagogy (Ackerley, Guarda and Helm, 2017a). The fact that lecturers feel confident communicating about their discipline in English aligns with their prevalent view of EMI as not involving any focus on language to facilitate students' learning of disciplinary communication – i.e. situated at the furthest end of the continuum of language versus content (Airey, 2016). In the Catalan context, where one of the main drivers of EMI is precisely to help students learn disciplinary language (referred to as CLIL-*ised* EMI by Moncada-Comas and Block, 2019), this lack of attention to language appears somehow contradictory.

Language challenges for EMI students include listening skills (Hellekjær 2010), understanding specialist vocabulary (Li and Ruan, 2015), reading specialised texts, and oral production (Doiz, Costa, Lasagabaster and Mariotti, 2019), increase in study burden (Tatzl, 2011), anxiety over class participation (Lei and Hu, 2014) and an overall inadequate linguistic competence (Doiz, Lasagabaster and Sierra, 2013). Nevertheless, comparisons of academic achievement among Spanish students taking the same course in L1 and EMI have shown no detrimental effect of EMI on academic performance (Dafouz and Camacho-Miñano, 2016).

The second strand relates to participants' motivations and personal responses to EMI. Age and English proficiency account for differences in lecturers' alignment with EMI and sense of agency – young teachers with a PhD stay abroad seem more willing to volunteer than older generations (Dearden and Macaro, 2016). Research has also shown lecturers' lack of awareness of the impact of their classes on students' development of disciplinary discourse (Arnó-Macià and Mancho-Barés, 2015) – though EMI has the potential to promote students' disciplinary literacies development (Zhang and Chan, 2017) – as well as the need to change their teaching behaviour (Bradford, 2019; Dearden and Macaro, 2016; Dimova and Kling, 2018). The conclusion is that teacher identity remains the same, i.e., that of an expert content lecturer who is internationally active and for whom using the specialised terminology in English is more natural than in their L1 (Dimova and Kling, 2018). Students' main motivations toward EMI include learning specialised vocabulary and practising or improving their English skills, along with studying/thinking in English (Ackerley, 2017; Aguilar, 2012; Dimova, Hultgren and Kling, 2015; Doiz et al., 2019; Guarda, 2018).

This study

This chapter focuses on the reasons why participants choose EMI or L1 teaching (in this case, Catalan) and, ensuing from that, the role of language in teaching advanced disciplinary knowledge. Attention is paid to the language-related concerns that participants identify, namely; (i) the role of language in choosing EMI or the L1; (ii) stakeholders' (viz. lecturer and students) views on the role of EMI at university; and (iii) views on English as either a tool for empowerment or as a barrier to discussing advanced disciplinary material. Accordingly, this chapter seeks to answer the following research questions:

RQ1. What makes students and lecturers choose English or L1 for an advanced disciplinary course?
RQ2. What effect(s) does the change from L1 to English have on the teaching of advanced disciplinary knowledge? Specifically:
  1) Do participants perceive any benefits (or losses) in terms of language or content in the change to EMI?
  2) Do participants hold any specific views on the learning and use of English for disciplinary communication?
RQ3. What are participants' views on EMI implementation?

Data

The subjects in the study are the lecturer and the students, and our main data come from semi-structured interviews, six with students from both classes (EMI: 3; L1: 3) and one with the lecturer.

The lecturer, Alberto,[2] was 35 years old and had just completed his PhD at the time of data collection. He is bilingual in Spanish and Catalan (although he has Spanish as his mother tongue and uses Catalan as his teaching/academic language at university). Because in this bilingual context speakers often switch between Spanish and Catalan, both languages are considered L1 in this study. At the time of data collection, Alberto had two years' experience in the Electronics Department, he had carried out two PhD stays abroad, and regularly used English as an academic language. He had self-selected for lecturing in English, and it was his third semester as an EMI lecturer. The six students interviewed self-selected to participate after the lecturer had asked for volunteers among those students who regularly attended classes (although Alberto did not know if these students were especially good at electronics because they had not been tested yet). Interview data were complemented with a survey inquiring into EMI and L1 students' perspectives about teaching and learning advanced disciplinary content, and was administered in paper format during one of the L1 and EMI class sessions. A total of 63 surveys (L1: 48; EMI: 15) were collected. The disparity in respondents in both groups reflects the different class sizes.

Survey

The survey, which was administered in Catalan, contained a demographic section (personal, linguistic, and international background) followed by ten questions dealing with a wide range of aspects that can help compare a parallel course in EMI and L1, namely reasons for choosing the course, previous experience with languages (and ESP in particular), perceived difficulty and learning outcomes, satisfaction and perceived quality, among others. In addition to the survey, the exam marks were also collected as a benchmark against which the students' perceived learning outcomes could be gauged. The survey was framed as follows. The first question was open-ended (e.g. *Why did you enrol in the Catalan/EMI group?*) and the rest were closed. Among these, all but the question on whether students had followed an ESP course (a 'yes/no' question) were Likert-type closed questions eliciting an evaluation of a number of aspects, such as perceived learning outcomes, perceived difficulty, and perceived linguistic readiness, e.g. *The lecturer's explanations are clear (fully disagree) 1 – 2 – 3 – 4 – 5 (fully agree)*. The questions analysed for this chapter were: *Reasons for enrolling in the L1 vs. EMI class*, *Perceptions of learning*, *Perceived difficulty of the course*, *Perceived readiness towards EMI*, *Previous ESP experience/views on ESP as preparation for EMI*, and *Satisfaction with L1 vs. EMI class*.

Interviews with participants

The interviews were carried out by the researchers – ESP lecturers at the same university, one of whom was an ESP lecturer in the school, recognised by participants as an ESP/language expert. The electronics lecturer interview took place at the end of the semester, while students were interviewed in the middle of the semester, which allowed researchers to ask about specific practices observed in lectures. Student interviews were individual, except one that was held with two students simultaneously. All interviews were carried out in Catalan and were transcribed verbatim, using orthographic transcription conventions – rather than phonetic symbols – as we were interested in the contents. For international readability, the extracts in this chapter have been translated into English by the researchers. A general set of questions was used for both types of participants to elicit their views on the different topics included in the survey: (i) personal reasons for choosing either English or Catalan as the medium of instruction (e.g. why did you enrol in the EMI/

Catalan class?), language-related concerns and challenges, perceptions about the course and specific methodology for EMI vs. L1 teaching (do you think that the fact that it is in English affects students' participation in class?), and perceived benefits; (ii) general views on EMI and institutional policies (Should there be more EMI courses at university?).

Analysis

The interviews were analysed thematically, through an inductive process (Saldaña, 2016), to identify the main topics (codes) by which participants referred to the foci of this study. Those codes were then grouped thematically: e.g. *schedule/ no more option* (theme: schedule); *prefer L1/ understand more in L1* (theme: better in L1). In contrast with the students' general comments, the lecturer delved into a reflection on his own practices, in what resulted in a conversation on EMI implementation. Sharing McCormack's (2000, p. 283) '[concern] that the traditional method of coding for themes in transcripts and studying those themes separated people's words from their spoken and heard context', we felt that the instructor's interview analysis could be constructed as a narrative (Johnson and Golombek, 2002), as he discursively made sense of his own teaching practices and reflected on his more general views on EMI. Thus, the general themes presented in the analysis are interpreted in the light of the dialogue between an EMI lecturer and the ESP researchers.

As background data, the survey analysis compared the responses of the EMI (n=15) vs. the L1 class (n=48). Quantitative analysis involved calculating the means and standard deviations for closed survey questions (with Minitab software) and a non-parametric Mann-Whitney test was used to identify any significant differences between both groups. The disparity of groups (as students self-selected to attend either class) means that the numbers should be taken with caution, given the small number of students in the EMI class.

The open-ended question in the survey was analysed qualitatively. The analysis of interviews with different participants aimed at unveiling possible contradictions and tensions in parallel EMI-L1 teaching, while the survey, as background data, helped contextualise and provide a richer account of the findings.

Findings

Survey

Students' age range was 22–26 (EMI) and 21–29 (L1), mostly male, as reflected across the whole programme, and both groups can be considered to have at least an upper-intermediate level of English (B2 according to the

Common European Framework of Reference for Languages, CEFR). The survey results are summarised in Table 2.1, focusing on the reasons for choosing EMI/L1, perceptions of learning, difficulty/readiness, and satisfaction.

The main reason for choosing English or the L1 appears to be a convenient schedule (EMI: 40%; L1: 77%). However, a few EMI students (20%) refer to the teaching quality of the lecturer and the motivation to learn technical English (13.3%), while L1 students do not mention the teacher, and almost a quarter of the students (22.9%) refer to the language challenge involved in EMI. Given the disparity in student numbers, we wanted to unveil the real reasons for language choice, although a convenient schedule is a plausible reason, as many masters' students have part-time jobs and prefer a later schedule (L1 class). The outstanding quality of the lecturer was highlighted by students in Aguilar and Arnó (2020), and may also have influenced the EMI choice. Given the low numbers, we wondered how many students would have chosen EMI had it not been for a lecturer with such a good reputation.

As seen in Table 2.1, while perceived learning outcomes are similar (and positive) for both groups, EMI students report learning both content *and* language (Ackerley, 2017; Doiz et al., 2019). Notably, they perceive that the move to EMI is not detrimental to learning, although the self-selection component has likely borne on students' feeling of having rightly chosen

Table 2.1 Survey findings for both groups.

Question	L1	EMI	
2. How much do you think you're learning in this course in terms of discipline content (electronics)?	3.65 (*SD 1.02*)	3.57 (*SD 1.45*)	p=0.96
3. How much do you think you're learning in this course in terms of English language?	n/a	3.23 (*SD 1.47*)	
5. Indicate the degree of difficulty of the course	3.83 (*SD 0.66*)	3.69 (*SD 1.47*)	p=0.30
6. To what extent do you feel you would be linguistically prepared to take this course in English?	3.94 (*SD 0.95*)	n/a	
7. Do you think that an ESP course would help you towards an/this EMI course?	3.70 (*SD 1.27*)	3.09 (*SD 1.53*)	p=0.08
8. So far I feel satisfied with the course	3.40 (*SD 1.17*)	4.00 (*SD 1.78*)	p=0.07
9. The lecturer's explanations are clear	4.26 (*SD 1.25*)	4.08 (*SD 2.02*)	p=0.78
10. I think the lecturer is good	4.47 (*SD 1.08*)	4.25 (*SD 1.92*)	p=0.31

EMI (Hellekjaer, 2007). The situation might have been different if EMI had been the only option available. L1 students report being linguistically ready for EMI, which points to a high perception of their level of proficiency. Similarly, both groups consider the course difficult (cf. Hellekjaer, 2010). However, the fact that L1 students express the need for an ESP course to support EMI may indicate a lower degree of self-confidence – and the perception of linguistic challenges – in contrast with EMI students. In terms of satisfaction, both the course and the lecturer were rated highly, with EMI students expressing a higher level of satisfaction, as they have succeeded in an EMI course. This sense of achievement can be corroborated with the final marks obtained, which were very similar for both groups: L1 (M=4.69, SD=1.8) and EMI (M=4.5, SD=1.6). This would suggest (despite the difference in class size) that EMI does not have a detrimental effect on learning (Dafouz and Camacho-Miñano, 2016).

Overall, survey results echo Doiz et al.'s (2019) and Guarda's (2018), in that EMI learning outcomes and difficulty are not perceived to differ significantly from L1 teaching.

Lecturer's interview

Choosing the language of instruction

This is a case of grassroots EMI implementation, based on the lecturer's self-selection and initiative. His account of the reasons for choosing EMI indicates a positive attitude ('let's do it', 'thrilled') towards a challenge (Extract 1):

> Yes, they told me that in previous years, when I wasn't there, he [coordinator] was lecturing in English and that besides you [researchers] were interested in that, and I said, look, let's do it in English because I feel capable, it is a challenge right? Lecturing in English is an extra effort, right? I don't feel as comfortable as in Catalan or Spanish but, well let's do it and very thrilled, yes, yes.
>
> (Extract 1)

A topic related to self-selection is that of self-confidence in English, although he acknowledges that he feels 'capable' but '[less] comfortable' than in the L1. Identifying English as the disciplinary language of electronics (Extract 2), he develops the idea of different levels of self-perceived competence in the technical register in contrast to everyday English (Extract 3):

> Because, well, because first of all I think that it is fundamental for a lecturer to master a foreign language and nowadays it's English, so being

able to lecture in English and feeling, let's say, at ease and besides the challenge of speaking and doing it in English…I like it.

(Extract 2)

I feel on a technical level very comfortable speaking and having a conversation but possibly face-to-face, that's exactly what you're saying, making a joke in English, I'm not feeling so comfortable. Sometimes I do try [telling jokes] or maybe I tell a joke, but I don't realise I'm doing it, but I feel that in this register I lack vocabulary and resources.

(Extract 3)

Alberto appears as a confident lecturer with a high self-perceived level of academic/technical English and satisfaction of succeeding in EMI, while he acknowledges a certain lack of nuance and spontaneity in casual interactions (Dimova, et al., 2015; Guarda and Helm, 2017a).

Views on EMI implementation

Alberto also expresses his position towards EMI implementation, including specific actions and university policies as well as more deeply grounded perceptions on the role of EMI. He seems to regard EMI as an option for lecturers, who can choose between English, Catalan and Spanish, rather than a planned institutional policy. This lecturer profile, a young scholar who is already used to working in English in academia, is aligned with the profiles of lecturers who opt for EMI (Unterberger, 2014). Self-selection facilitates EMI implementation, with motivated lecturers acting as 'agents of change' (Dearden and Macaro, 2016). On the other hand, given student self-selection based on language learning motivations, institutions should take measures accordingly, for example, by providing language support (Hellekjaer, 2007).

The lecturer's views align with the EMI driver of improving students' proficiency (in contrast to increasing the internationalisation profile of the institution). Thus, EMI becomes both a scenario for immersion in discipline-specific communication and a challenge, as students have to '*make [an] effort to adapt to the [disciplinary] world in English*'. Alberto's view of EMI implementation is that of adding value to teaching, as EMI helps students towards disciplinary English communication, necessary in the professional world:

Well, I think so, anything that means facing, I think we have to consider their professional world, in the future they'll find English, I think we have to take into account their future professional world […] Will they find English or not? Of course they'll find English, a lot, so if they make this effort to adapt to the world in English during their study years at the university, well it's advantageous.

(Extract 4)

Along these lines, he also specifies that EMI should be implemented 'gradually', to facilitate students' adaptation to an English-speaking environment:

And if it can be gradual, gradually following one or two courses in English or if they can approach and ask the lecturer if they don't understand something, if they have to, I think it's much better this way, at the university, and gradually, let's say, in an adaptive way rather than suddenly when they first enter the professional world.

(Extract 5)

In Extract 5, resonating with Hellekjaer (2007), 'adaptive' emerges as a keyword, suggesting the idea of scaffolding, a view that somehow contradicts actual EMI implementation, which depends on the lecturer's individual initiative rather than on a planned institutional strategy. Precisely, on reconciling top-down policies and bottom-up implementations, Airey, Lauridsen, Räsänen, Salö, and Schwach (2017) suggest including disciplinary language learning skills as part of EMI course goals, in line with institutional policies that acknowledge disciplinary differences. Such an approach to disciplinary literacies, however, would be best approached from an ESP-content lecturer collaboration 'for the effective induction of students into the practices and discourses of the disciplines' (Zhang and Chan, 2017, p. 142).

Teaching methodology and EMI

According to his view of EMI as a mere language switch, Alberto uses a technical metaphor, describing language as *'the output interface'*. His view matches Airey's (2016) definition of EMI, situated at the end of the continuum between EAP at one extreme (exclusive focus on language), an intermediate CLIL (focus on content *and* language), and at the other extreme, EMI (exclusive focus on content). His approach does not entail any methodological change, on the grounds that a good lecturer in the L1 is also good in EMI (Aguilar and Arnó, 2020). The contradiction that appears is that EMI requires a certain language focus, as the lecturer needs to adapt teaching to cater for students with different proficiency levels. A more apt term for this scenario is the recently proposed concept of *'CLIL-ised EMI'* (Moncada-Comas and Block, 2019). The compartmentalisation of content and language implied by Alberto reflects a somehow antagonistic view of content versus language (Airey, 2012) that does not align with his previous comments on language problems caused by EMI, nor does it align with the concept of English acting as a bridge or cognitive pathway in EMI (Hellekjaer and Wilkinson, 2003):

> So, if I draw on my experience, I'd say you don't need to do anything extra. I'd say in my opinion simply explain concepts in English and that's it […] if you explain well in Catalan you'll do, be, the same lecturer in Catalan as in English.
>
> (Extract 6)

Thus, Alberto's view that the only requisite for EMI is language proficiency, while effective pedagogy can be transferred to EMI, is reinforced by the assertion that master's students are linguistically ready for EMI ('*they have the right level to cope with classes in English and teaching in English*'). Another apparent (and subtle) contradiction is between the view of EMI as a mere language change and the need for pedagogical adaptations. The fact that he gives such an elaborated explanation, which leads him to contradict himself, may be influenced by the lecturer's and researchers' roles: on the one hand, an electronics lecturer who is highly motivated towards EMI and towards sharing his experience by participating in the present study, and on the other, two ESP lecturers (one of them from the same school) recognised by the electronics lecturer as experts in academic/technical English, EMI, and university pedagogy. This situation may have led the lecturer not only to present his personal views, but also to construct his own narrative through the dialogic construction of knowledge during the interview (Johnson and Golombek, 2002), in a situation that he probably regards (judging from his interest in the research) as the opportunity to verbalise his practices and beliefs on EMI as part of his professional growth.

Two contradictions can be found to the view that EMI requires no adaptation. First, it contrasts with the previous idea of scaffolding – and gradual introduction of EMI – at bachelor's level. Second, a closer look into the differences between EMI and L1 teaching unveils the lecturer's idea of EMI as a challenge for students as, when offered the choice between EMI and L1, only the 'brave' students choose English. In relation to the disparity of class sizes, Alberto acknowledges the extra complexity that EMI adds to an already complex course.

Lecturer: maybe, yes, they have to make a little effort, I think that this is reflected in the number of students that we have in the English group
Interviewer: you think you've got fewer students because they're the brave ones, as it were.

Lecturer: exactly, I think they know they have to make this little effort to attend a course in English but they're brave enough to say 'I can face electronics' which has traditionally been difficult. They don't like electronics but on top of that they dare follow it in English and they do that without fear.

(Extract 7)

The role of language(s) in EMI

The lecturer delves into his use of different languages in the preparation/ delivery of his classes. First, the fact that English is widely used in academia reinforces his view of EMI as a mere switch to 'explaining concepts in English'. In a discipline such as electronics, this change is seen as a less challenging task given the widespread presence of English in the discipline. Like the science lecturers in Dimova and Kling (2018), Alberto is used to dealing with disciplinary content in English, which he even uses in his L1 classes.

> Even in the Catalan lecture, concepts in English arose, so I don't think it's so complicated to make the move to English, especially if you've got experience, you've attended conferences and you write papers in English in your field.

(Extract 8)

A somewhat surprising finding about the lecturer's day-to-day practices was that in a course taught in parallel in Catalan and English, the classes had originally been prepared in a different language, Spanish. This move between the three languages aligns with the university's policy towards trilingualism (i.e. adding English to the two working languages of the community).[3]

> Yes, really, and in fact I already had everything prepared from the last semester when I lectured in Spanish. In fact, I've got everything in Spanish, so, yes.

(Extract 9)

Upon further inquiry into whether he translated from Spanish to English and Catalan, he clarified that his preparation did not involve translation, but rather reformulation (i.e. *'expressing concepts in English'*). This move across languages merits further attention. The fact that the course materials (slides, videos, and software) are originally in English indicates the complexity of moving to EMI, which the lecturer refers to by pointing out that he is not 'translating', but reformulating. Apparently, this move across

Language issues in EMI 31

languages (Extract 10) involves taking a concept originally in English (literature, materials) for which he had prepared formulations in Spanish (when he first prepared the course) and reformulating it in Catalan – quite easily for a bilingual speaker – as well as in English, the latter involving a more complex process of explaining, in perhaps simpler language, but in any case with greater effort. He hints at these ongoing processes of on-the-spot reformulations when he acknowledges that the verbal explanations (which he writes on the blackboard) differ from the ones previously written in his notebook. Accordingly, such complex processes of (re)formulation across languages seem to contradict Alberto's stated view of EMI as a mere language switch.

Interviewer: you translate from Spanish to English and from Spanish to Catalan
Lecturer: it's not exactly translating either. It's reading the concept and saying ok, this is the concept and I write it on the blackboard and in fact if we compare the blackboard with my notebook it's never the same concept.
(Extract 10)

In sum, a highly confident young scholar with good English and teaching skills, Alberto decided to teach one of his classes in English, probably to give his students experience in technical/academic English. Apart from the reflection that master's students are linguistically ready for EMI, he does not express awareness of the level of students or the possible linguistic challenges that they may face. He probably thinks that through exposure, they will learn technical English. This assumption can be challenged from multiple perspectives. On the one hand, a context in which EMI is considered a means to 'teach' technical English would call for planned language support (one of the 'lost opportunities' identified by Hellekjaer, 2007). On the other hand, the complexities found in the lecturer's views (adapting content to students' linguistic level) and reported practices across languages (reformulations), and how these stand in contradiction with his stated view of English as the '*output interface*' merit closer examination.

Students' interviews

Choosing the language of instruction

Regarding the choice of language, we were interested in examining the disparity in class sizes (L1: 71; EMI: 15), which, in the survey, was explained by schedule convenience. Yet, we wondered whether language had an effect, which is why we paid special attention to the reasons expressed in the interviews. Actually, both L1 and EMI students confirmed schedule convenience, and although they did not explicitly acknowledge the role of language, they voiced some kind of reservation about EMI.

> I saw it was in Catalan; it was to adjust my class schedule, right? I didn't choose it because it was in Catalan or in English. But if I had seen that it was in English maybe I'd have reconsidered [doing it in Catalan].
> (Student 1 – L1 – Extract 11)

Another L1 student reflects on his experience, as he acknowledges, in hindsight, that he would not have had any problems with EMI, since the L1 class materials are already in English. This would indicate a possible way of gradually introducing EMI, by incorporating parts of the materials in English (Arnó-Macià and Aguilar-Pérez, 2018), which can encourage students towards EMI.

> Now I think I could have done it in English and I wouldn't have had much trouble because, besides, many documents, if not all documents, they upload are in English.
> (Student 2 – L1 –Extract 12)

When asked about his choice, the following EMI student also mentions timetable. In fact, he did not know the class was in English until the first lesson, but he decided to stay because of the good lecturer, a remark that resonates with the lecturer's view on effective pedagogy being transferrable across languages.

> No, I enrolled in the schedule that best suited me and I arrived the first day and saw it was in English and, as I liked the teacher, how he taught, I decided to stay.
> (Student 6 – EMI – Extract 13)

In sum, although most students claim to have chosen EMI or L1 because of their schedule, when asked directly, certain underlying criteria are unveiled, which can be used to foster the progressive implementation of EMI through the use of materials in English in the L1 class and the use of effective lecturing styles. Both actions could lessen the perception of difficulty.

Language mediating disciplinary knowledge

According to students, there were no substantial differences in their learning outcomes between the EMI and the L1 class. Alberto was considered *a good lecturer* (Aguilar and Arnó, 2020). As electronics is a difficult subject ('a beast'), good teaching skills seemed to have a more important role than language in helping students to understand complex contents. As shown in

Extract 14, EMI does not seem to be detrimental to learning, as the student reports learning both language and content (and immersion in English is seen as an added value). Interestingly enough, and maybe because it is an engineering subject, the student clearly separates the electronics concepts from the language of instruction.

> Apart from learning what he's teaching you, you're practising your English, which is also good. I mean, the fact it's in English is an added value…I don't have problems in understanding concepts or later in studying them because at the end of the day concepts are neither in English nor in Catalan. So, what he's teaching you is how those concepts work.
> (Student 6 – EMI – Extract 14)

In the evaluation of the subject's difficulty, it is important to consider that it involves practical, problem-solving work. Thus, similar to the perceptions of the students analysed in Kim, Kweon, and Kim (2017), our EMI students feel that problem-based engineering courses do not pose as much of a challenge as would other disciplines that require extensive writing or argumentation.

> It's only problems, so actually the words you have to learn, the difficulty does not lie in cramming or writing a text…it's being able to solve problems and there are many words that are in English: bits, bytes, in Catalan they're the same words.
> (Student 4 – EMI – Extract 15)

In contrast with EMI students, who feel satisfied with the idea of learning content and language and find no language barriers, the following L1 student is more sceptical about the introduction of EMI, which should have been introduced in earlier stages, and ideally involving less complex subject matter.

> Me, Catalan. But like I said, if there had been some progression like in the bachelor's if we'd already had several courses in English so that we got into it, …nice, right?
> (Student 1 – L1 – Extract 16)

Language improvement through EMI

Following participants' view of EMI as a scenario for (disciplinary) language learning, one of the topics that emerge is that of perceived language improvement. The student below explicitly acknowledges that he has chosen EMI in order to learn ('*get used to*') technical English.

Interviewer: if there was another EMI course in the master's, would you take it?
Student: I would, because I must get into technical English, above all that's the reason, to get used to technical English.

(Student 5 – EMI – Extract 17)

The following L1 student also considers EMI as a way of learning English. In this case, she regrets not having taken EMI. Disregarding the possibility of undertaking any formal language instruction, she thinks that the extensive practice involved in EMI (reading, listening, and speaking in English) could have helped her towards the exam that she now has to take. She aligns herself with the two usual institutional aims of EMI, internationalisation and (especially) language development.

> Now I gotta do one of these exams for one of these placement tests and I think 'gosh if I had spent all this time studying in English and speaking in English, listening to a teacher in English, I'd hardly have any problem in doing it'…Plus, orally presenting some work and also if everything is in English that'd make you do it in English too and, it's good for this reason, for internationalising the school too.

(Student 3 – L1 – Extract 18)

As EMI is considered a way of learning technical English, one wonders why ESP courses are only mentioned by one student (incidentally, the only student with ESP experience). She reflects on the use of English in her job and positions herself in favour of ESP courses designed to prepare students for professional communication.

> When I started your [ESP] course, I thought it was something that shouldn't be optional…I was in a company that, well…it makes boarding x [inaudible] for well harbours and airports and well, you do projects for all around the world and when I was at the Sales department, but it was technical because I had to try and sell them things that were technical, giving specifications, writing technical things…It was when I said to myself 'it doesn't matter what you've done, it's much more important that the things you know you can communicate them properly in English'.

(Student 3 – L1 – Extract 19)

In sum, students regard EMI as the acquisition of new concepts and specialist vocabulary in English, which is a similar position to that held by the lecturer (Pecorari et al., 2011; Dimova and Kling, 2018). In either case, an idea that is quite widespread among all students is that EMI is a way of learning technical English, even if the course does not include any language learning goals (Aguilar, 2012; Moncada-Comas and Block, 2019).

EMI implementation

Some of the views expressed by students helped shed light on conditions for implementation, namely types of courses appropriate for EMI, teaching practices, and barriers to implementation.

This EMI student hints at electronics being an appropriate course for EMI, given the pervasive use of English-based material. One of the advantages of EMI is that students gain fluency through extensive practice, which in turn helps them cope with disciplinary material in English (a need beyond EMI).

> This weekend I was doing some activities we have, it's some videos, it's for all the groups alike, Catalan groups too. The last two topics you don't do them in class, you gotta watch the videos, and they're in English, and I thought, good, I wasn't translating…I was studying in English, that is, writing the ideas on the video and I thought 'well, this is the same for everyone'.
> (Student 4 – EMI – Extract 20)

In relation to teaching practices, scaffolding is considered a good practice which helps to lower the linguistic barrier and make complex disciplinary content more manageable. As shown in the reported practices below, Alberto uses a high degree of explicit teaching and redundancy.

> He writes a lot, but on the blackboard. That is, he is explaining everything. In this subject people complained because PowerPoint slides aren't very useful…then he does this on the blackboard; he's keen on writing notes, like five important notes and then you have this in English.
> (Student 4 – EMI – Extract 21)

Possible barriers to EMI implementation include students' lack of experience using English as an academic language as well as lecturers' linguistic readiness. EMI courses must be 'well prepared', which goes beyond the basic requisite of lecturers' proficiency and includes strategies like scaffolding '*technical vocabulary*'. Extract 22 summarises such requisites, namely gradual exposure to discipline-related English skills. This view is expressed by an L1 student, who is rather sceptical about EMI, as he shows some need for language support (cf. Doiz et al., 2019).

Yes, [lecturer's proficiency level] it's the basics, that is, if the person who's gonna teach you has a lower English level than you, well, it's complicated and then, look, to implement it gradually. I don't know, I'm now thinking of extra material on technical vocabulary, that they give you a short form and that's it, as easy as that...essentially, the lecturer and the materials.

(Student 1 – L1 – Extract 22)

Discussion and conclusion

In a course taught in parallel in EMI and the L1, this chapter has aimed at unveiling participants' reasons for choosing the language of instruction, views on the role of language in mediating disciplinary content, and EMI implementation. The answer to RQ1, *reasons for choosing EMI or L1 teaching*, reveals some tensions. Although the survey yields the apparent reason of schedule convenience, students admit to also considering the challenge involved in EMI. The disparity in class sizes indicates the existence of other hidden reasons, confirmed by the analysis of the interviews (Extracts #5, #7, #11, #12, #13, #15, #16). The lecturer acknowledges that English increases the complexity of a highly difficult course, which affects student numbers. Students, on the other hand, call for a more systematic implementation of EMI, moving from less to more complex subject matter. Both coincide in the need for a clear EMI policy, since current EMI implementation as a grassroots initiative based on self-selection stands in contradiction with undefined general university policies (Dafouz-Milne, Camacho-Miñano and Urquía-Grande, 2014). Considering that this course was implemented on the lecturer's initiative, relying on his self-confidence and high level of proficiency, it is not surprising to find students' reservations (especially among L1 students; Extracts #13, #16, #18). EMI students' self-selection is reflected in their positive perception and sense of achievement. In this context, the lecturer becomes an 'agent of change' (Dearden and Macaro, 2016) whose motivation and effective lecturing can help draw other lecturers towards EMI, although greater planning would be needed to make EMI implementation more systematic and gradual (Extracts #5, #16, #22).

Regarding RQ2, on the *effect of changing from L1 to English on the teaching of advanced disciplinary knowledge*, the move to EMI does *not* appear to have an effect either on learning outcomes or course satisfaction, with even a higher degree of satisfaction among the EMI students (probably due to their sense of achievement). As acknowledged by students, the practical and problem-based nature of the course makes it appropriate for EMI. Neither does language become a barrier, probably because it was a master's course taken by students with advanced language and content level – in contrast with the linguistic challenges that bachelor's students may face (Ackerley, 2017; Kim et al., 2017).

To answer the first sub-question related to perceived benefits, or losses, in language or content, students have the impressionistic feeling that EMI helps them develop their technical English (which to them mostly amounts to *specialised vocabulary*), and thus view EMI as an added value. Although most terminology is in English even in the L1 class, EMI provides an immersion context for students' extensive skills practice and a self-perceived gain in fluency (Extracts #14, #17, #20, #22). In any case, the extent to which such perceived language gains are produced is an issue that merits further research.

Both the lecturer and the students view EMI as a way of learning disciplinary English without being detrimental to learning electronics. Students, however, highlight that this is possible because of Alberto's good language and teaching skills, which yields a picture of successful EMI as a combination of personal, pedagogic and language skills (Tatzl, 2011; Rose, Curle, Aizawa and Thompson, 2019). The lecturer's stated view of EMI as a mere language shift (Airey, 2016) appears somehow contradictory with his own views of scaffolding and adapting (Extract #5, #6, #7, #9).

Focusing on learning English for disciplinary communication (sub-question #2), students agree that ESP courses would be welcome – as indicated by survey answers and by L1 students' expressed need for linguistic support (Extract #18). This is one of the discrepancies between the views of students, who suggest that EMI should be supported by language training (aligning with Jiang et al., 2019), and that of the lecturer, who believes that EMI students do not need any specific preparation beyond a given level of proficiency, as EMI will provide them with disciplinary language skills. From an ESP perspective, we wonder why despite widespread awareness of the need for English in the professional and academic world, there is a general lack of awareness of the existence and usefulness of ESP/EAP courses. Resonating with Thompson, Aizawa, Curle and Rose's (2019) findings that students perceive ESP preparation as beneficial for EMI, a case can be made for ESP courses for the development of disciplinary literacies. Students seem to regard technical English/language improvement as a by-product of EMI, requiring no formal or explicit teaching – maybe because language and content are envisioned as two separate entities.

Finally, the answer to RQ3 (*participants' views on EMI implementation*) unveils the contrast between loosely defined views of EMI that disregard students' linguistic hurdles and the role of ESP, including the lecturer's contradiction between a mere language change (Airey, 2016) and the need to be 'adaptive' (Hellekjaer, 2007), as well as the challenges, benefits and suggestions for EMI improvement made by students (Extracts #15, #18, #21).

Students voice two main challenges to EMI implementation, namely lack of planning and systematicity, and the ensuing need for scaffolding disciplinary language learning. Regarding planning and systematicity, the views gathered can become useful points of departure, such as the choice of problem-solving courses based on numerical information as especially appropriate for EMI, provided teaching skills and a sound proficiency level are satisfactory and students can choose the language of instruction. Gradual implementation also appears to be an appropriate guideline which is, together with the factors involved in self-selection (i.e. what makes lecturers and students choose EMI) discussed below.

The second, and main, challenge to EMI implementation relates to how students can be best prepared for disciplinary language learning. Even if EMI lecturers refuse to teach language (Airey, 2012; Doiz et al., 2019), this 'CLIL-ised EMI' context (Moncada-Comas and Block, 2019) calls for some kind of systematic attention to language and disciplinary communication. The lecturer's stated view of EMI aimed at improving domestic students' disciplinary English stands in contradiction with the expectation that this development will result from mere exposure (Dearden and Macaro, 2016). In sum, the exploration of participants' motivations has disclosed tensions between intrinsic (e.g. challenge, previous familiarity with academic English) and extrinsic motivations (e.g. preparing for the professional world). Similarly, EMI also appears as an option for young lecturers, like the one in this study, who are used to using English as an academic language, and whose motivation leans more towards helping students learn disciplinary English than towards contributing to the institution's internationalisation strategy. It is precisely this motivation that can serve as a springboard for enhancing collaboration between content and ESP experts, taking disciplinary literacies – the unveiled driver of EMI in this study – as the point of departure (Zhang and Chan, 2017). Hopefully, a study like this one, unveiling the views, practices, and concerns that EMI lecturers and students share with ESP lecturers can be a step forward in that direction. Such dialogues can help enhance content lecturers' awareness of students' linguistic skills and needs. Lecturers like Alberto, who have had to use English in their academic work, assume that disciplinary English can be learned through informal exposure (cf. Pecorari et al., 2011) and may not be aware of students' need for ESP. In contrast, in another study set in the same context, where students were specifically asked about ESP, they considered it good preparation for academic communication in general and EMI in particular (Arnó Aguilar and Taztl, 2020), a finding that resonates with Unterberger's (2014) study.

Despite the limitations of such a small-scale study, the in-depth analysis of a particular course offered in parallel in the L1 and EMI has unveiled some contradictions that form part of the 'secret life' of EMI. In other

Language issues in EMI 39

words, when participants are free to choose between embarking on EMI or staying in their L1 comfort zone, it is useful to delve into the underlying motivations. Only by listening to them can we confront shared or contradictory perceptions among lecturers and students. Studies like this one shed light on the complex and hidden realities that sometimes lie underneath the large figures that may paint a smooth picture of the internationalisation of universities and their alleged adherence to a growing EMI trend.

Notes

1 All data cited in this chapter is from the project *Towards an empirical assessment of the impact of English-medium instruction at university: language learning, disciplinary knowledge and academic identities* (ASSEMID), funded by the Spanish Ministry of Economy, Industry and Competitiveness (*El Ministerio de Economía, Industria y Competitividad* – MINECO), code FFI2016-76383-P. 30 December 2016 – 29 December 2019.
2 A pseudonym.
3 The UPC language policy (n.d.) states: 'The UPC is a multilingual university whose working languages are Catalan, Spanish and English.'

References

Ackerley, K. (2017). What the students can teach us about EMI and language issues. In K. Ackerley, M. Guarda & F. Helm (Eds.), *Sharing perspectives on English-medium instruction* (pp. 257–284). Bern: Peter Lang Publishing.

Aguilar, M., & Rodríguez, R. (2012). Lecturer and student perceptions on CLIL at a Spanish university. *International Journal of Bilingual Education and Bilingualism*, *15*(2), 183–197.

Aguilar, M., & Arnó, E. (2020). 'He's a good lecturer in any language': Shifting from L1 to English and implications for EMI training. In M. Mar Sánchez-Pérez (Ed.), *Teacher training for English medium instruction in higher education* (pp. 153–178). Hershey, PA: IGI-Global.

Airey, J. (2012). 'I don't teach language.' The linguistic attitudes of physics lecturers in Sweden. *AILA Review*, *25*, 64–79.

Airey, J. (2016). EAP, EMI or CLIL? In K. Hyland & P. Shaw (Eds.), *The Routledge handbook of English for academic purposes* (pp. 71–83). London: Routledge.

Airey, J., Lauridsen, K. M., Räsänen, A., Salö, L., & Schwach, V. (2017). The expansion of English-medium instruction in the Nordic countries: Can top-down university language policies encourage bottom-up disciplinary literacy goals? *The International Journal of Higher Education Research*, *73*(4), 561–576.

Arnó-Macià, E., Aguilar-Pérez, M., & Tatzl, D. (2020). Engineering students' perceptions of the role of ESP courses in internationalized universities. *English for Specific Purposes*, *58*, 58–74.

Arnó-Macià, E., & Aguilar-Pérez, M. (2018). ESP, EMI and interculturality: How internationalised are university curricula in Catalonia? *ESP Today*, *6*(2), 184–207.

Arnó-Macià, E., & Mancho-Barés, G. (2015). The role of content and language in content and language integrated learning (CLIL) at university: Challenges and implications for ESP. *English for Specific Purposes, 37*, 63–73.

Ball, P., & Lindsay, D. (2013). Language demands and support for English-medium instruction in tertiary education: Learning from a specific context. In A. Doiz, D. Lasagabaster & J. M. Sierra (Eds.), *English-medium instruction at universities: Global challenges* (pp. 44–61). Bristol: Multilingual Matters.

Bradford, A. (2019). 'It's not all about English!' The problem of language foregrounding in English-medium instruction programmes in Japan. *Journal of Multilingual and Multicultural Development, 40*(8), 707–720.

Clark, C. (2017). Perceptions of EMI: The students' view of a master's degree programme. In K. Ackerley, M. Guarda & F. Helm (Eds.), *Sharing perspectives on English-medium instruction* (pp. 285–308). Bern: Peter Lang Publishing.

Dafouz, E., & Camacho-Miñano, M. (2016). Exploring the impact of English-medium instruction on university student academic achievement: The case of accounting. *English for Specific Purposes, 44*, 57–67.

Dafouz-Milne, E., Camacho-Miñano, M., & Urquía-Grande, E. (2014). 'Surely they can't do as well': A comparison of business students' academic performance in English-medium instruction and Spanish-as-first-language-medium programs. *Language and Education, 28*, 223–236.

Dearden, J., & Macaro, E. (2016). Higher education teachers' attitudes towards English medium instruction: A three-country comparison. *Studies in Second Language Learning and Teaching, 6*(3), 455–486.

Dimova, S., Hultgren, K., & Kling, J. (Eds.). (2015). *English-medium instruction in European higher education*. Berlin: Walter de Gruyter.

Dimova, S., & Kling, J. (2018). Assessing English-medium instruction lecturer language proficiency across disciplines. *TESOL Quarterly, 52*(3), 634–656.

Doiz, A., Costa, F., Lasagabaster, D., & Mariotti, C. (2019). Linguistic demands and language assistance in EMI courses. What is the stance of Italian and Spanish undergraduates? *Lingue e Linguaggi, 33*, 69–85.

Guarda, M. (2018). 'I just sometimes forget that I'm actually studying in English': Exploring student perceptions on English-Medium Instruction at an Italian university. *Rassegna Italiana di Linguistica Applicata (RILA), 2/3*, 129–144.

Guarda, M., & Helm, F. (2017a). A survey of lecturers' needs and feedback on EMI training. In K. Ackerley, M. Guarda & F. Helm (Eds.), *Sharing perspectives on English-medium instruction* (pp. 167–194). Bern: Peter Lang Publishing.

Guarda, M., & Helm, F. (2017b). 'I have discovered new teaching pathways': The link between language shift and teaching practice. *International Journal of Bilingual Education and Bilingualism, 20*(7), 897–913.

Hellekjær, G. O. (2007). The implementation of undergraduate level English medium programs in Norway: An exploratory case study. In R. Wilkinson & V. Zegers (Eds.), *Researching content and language integration in higher education* (pp. 68–81). Nijmegen & Maastricht: Valkhof Pers & Maastricht University.

Hellekjær, G. O. (2010). Assessing lecture comprehension in Norwegian English medium higher education. *Hermes, Journal of Language and Communication Studies, 45*, 11–27.
Hellekjær, G. O., & Wilkinson, R. (2003). Trends in content learning through English at universities: As critical reflection. (pp. 91–102). In C. Van Leeuwen & R. Wilkinson (Eds.), *Multilingual approaches in university education: Challenges and practices* (pp. 81–102). Maastricht: Universiteit Maastricht & Uitgeverij Valkhof Pers.
Jiang, L., Zhang, L. J., & May, S. (2019). Implementing English-medium instruction (EMI) in China: Teachers' practices and perceptions, and students' learning motivation and needs. *International Journal of Bilingual Education and Bilingualism, 22*(2), 107–119.
Johnson, K. E., & Golombek, P. R. (2002). Inquiry into experience: Teachers' personal and professional growth. In K. E. Johnson & P. R. Golombek (Eds.), *Teachers' narrative inquiry as professional development* (pp. 1–14). Cambridge: Cambridge University Press.
Kim, E. G., Kweon, S.-O., & Kim, J. (2017). Korean engineering students' perceptions on English-medium instruction and L1 use in EMI classes. *Journal of Multilingual and Multicultural Development, 38*(2), 130–145.
Lei, J., & Hu, G. (2014). Is English-medium instruction effective in improving Chinese undergraduate students' English competence? *International Review of Applied Linguistics and Language Teaching, 52*(2), 99–126.
Li, Ch., & Ruan, Z. (2015). Changes in beliefs about language learning among Chinese EAP learners in an EMI context in Mainland China: A socio-cultural perspective. *System, 55*, 43–52.
Macaro, E., Curle, S., Pun, J., An, J., & Dearden, J. (2018). A systematic review of English medium instruction in higher education. *Language Teaching, 51*(1), 36–76.
McCormack, C. (2000). From interview transcript to interpretative story: Part 1. Viewing the transcript through multiple lenses. *Field Methods, 12*(4), 282–297.
Moncada-Comas, B., & Block, D. (2019). CLIL-ised EMI in practice: Issues arising. *The Language Learning Journal*. doi:10.1080/09571736.2019.1660704.
Pecorari, D., Shaw, P., Irvine, A., & Malmström, M. (2011). English for academic purposes at Swedish universities: Teachers' objectives and practices. *Iberica, 22*, 55–77.
Rose, H., Curle, S., Aizawa, I., & Thompson, G. (2019). What drives success in English medium taught courses? The interplay between language proficiency, academic skills, and motivation. *Studies in Higher Education*. doi:10.1080/03075079.2019.1590690.
Saldaña, J. (2016). *The coding manual for qualitative researchers*. London: Sage Publishers.
Tatzl, D. (2011). English-medium masters' programmes at an Austrian university of applied sciences: Attitudes, experiences and challenges. *Journal of English for Academic Purposes, 10*(4), 252–270.

Thompson, G., Aizawa, I., Curle, S., & Rose, H. (2019). Exploring the role of self-efficacy beliefs and learner success in English medium instruction. *International Journal of Bilingual Education and Bilingualism*, *22*(1), 1–14.

Tsou, W., & Kao, Sh.-M. (Eds.). (2017). *English as a medium of instruction in higher education. Implementations and classroom practices in Taiwan.* Singapore: Springer.

Unterberger, B. (2014). English-medium degree programmes in Austrian tertiary business studies: Policies and programme design. Unpublished PhD dissertation. Retrieved July 28, 2020, from https://usearch.univie.ac.at/primo-explore/fulldisplay?docid=UWI_alma21321472280003332&context=L&vid=UWI&lang=de_DE.

UPC language policy (n.d.). Retrieved November 20, 2019, from https://www.upc.edu/slt/ca/servei-llengues-terminologia/pla-llengues-upc/pla-angles.

Zhang, Z., & Chan, E. (2017). Current research and practice in teaching disciplinary literacies. *ESP Today*, *5*(2), 132–147.

3 'Being a student' and 'doing education'

A multimodal analysis of *backstage* and *frontstage* interactional episodes in EMI[1]

Balbina Moncada-Comas

Introduction

In the course of her study of how to analyse multimodal interaction, Norris (2004, p. 2) suggests that sometimes 'gesture, gaze, and head movement also may take the superior position in a given interaction, while language may be subordinated or absent altogether'. Applying this view to the context of EMI, Morell (2018) explores a multimodal discourse analysis of how the multimodal ensembles of an EMI lecturer result in an effective pedagogy by involving students and eliciting meaning. However, students' multimodality also needs to be taken into account because an effective EMI pedagogy should consider students' behaviour in EMI classes in order to be more student-centred. In these classes, students confront disciplinary subject matter in a language other than their L1, and there is, as a result, space for multimodal resources to be used to compensate for any gaps in communicative competence. This chapter focuses on EMI students' use of semiotic resources and their multimodal ensembles. Using a multimodal methodology and applying Goffman's notions of 'frontstage' and 'backstage' to understand the classroom dynamics, this chapter seeks to answer the following research questions:

1) What specific multimodal resources do students use in *backstage* or *frontstage* interactions?
2) What subject positions – 'being a student' and/or 'doing education' – do students construct backstage or frontstage with multimodal resources?

The chapter is organised as follows. In the opening section I provide background information, discussing key concepts related to classroom interaction, in particular my use of Goffman's (1959) dramaturgical metaphor and Benwell and Stokoe's (2002) distinction between 'doing education' and 'being a student'. I then discuss the methodological framework, which draws on multimodality research. This done, in the second half of the chapter, I consider information about the research context and the informants and I discuss the analyses of a selected stretch of data from the class observed. I end the chapter with a consideration of what we have learned from this research, adding some general conclusions.

Theoretical background

In *The Presentation of Self in Everyday Life*, Erving Goffman (1959) suggests that in any social setting participants have certain knowledge about the situation they are in and about the other participants present. If the social setting at hand is a classroom setting, in particular an EMI classroom, both lecturer and students know that the situation is more formal than informal, what role they play in the situation, and why they are all there (i.e. the teaching and learning of disciplinary knowledge in English). In short, participants in a classroom setting know how to behave because they are aware of what is going on there, as they are engaged in the business of 'doing education' (Benwell and Stokoe, 2002). Just as 'people are constantly mobilizing their energies to create socially meaningful "impressions" (Meyrowitz, 1990, p. 68), students in a classroom also understand and recognise the social situation of which they are part. For this reason, learners also set, present, and convey a role of '*who*' they are in that particular context because they are 'able to acquire immediate sense of the overall structure of the situation and who is in what role' (Meyrowitz, 1990, p. 68).

The roles that people present in a social setting are, according to Goffman, 'performances'. As Meyrowitz (1990, p. 68) explains:

> Selected displays of behaviour that must, to some extent, consciously or unconsciously, be planned and rehearsed. In front of each of our audiences, we highlight certain aspects of ourselves and mute others. And, just as a play, the stage must be properly set, the actors must carefully control their actions, and the scripts for one drama must not be confused with scripts from other dramas

Elsewhere Burns (1992) notes how in *The Presentation of Self*, Goffman uses the metaphor of behaviour as stage performance to analyse how people manifest their conduct in society (see also Manning, 1992). Continuing with Goffman's dramaturgical metaphors, performances may be said to occur in two distinct settings – *frontstage* and *backstage*. Thornborrow and Haarman

(2012, p. 376) also make this distinction between stages, referring to them as 'two distinct social domains: the public and the private'. Frontstage refers to that behaviour performed in front of an audience. As Goffman puts it: 'the individual presents himself before others, his performance will tend to incorporate and exemplify the official accredited values' (1959, p. 35). Accordingly, frontstage behaviour often conforms to cultural expectations. Meanwhile, the backstage area is 'a space hidden from the audience and shared with others who perform the same and similar roles in relation to the audience' (Meyrowitz, 1990, p. 69). As Goffman (1959, p. 112) puts it, individuals in the backstage can 'drop their front' and 'step out of character'. Robinson and Schulz (2016, p. 57) characterise backstage talk as 'visceral narratives that challenge cultural expectations and fall out of alignment with honorable narratives expressed frontstage'. Individuals' images in the backstage may be 'incompatible with the image of themselves they are trying to convey' in the frontstage (Burns, 1992, p. 114). Therefore, Goffman's dramaturgical concepts of frontstage and backstage can also shed light on students' presentations of their selves in classroom contexts.

As one anonymous reviewer of an earlier draft of this chapter suggested, the classroom setting does not represent the same physical space as the theatre because students and teachers cannot physically move in and out of the front region and the back region. While I acknowledge this difference between a theatre and a classroom, I nonetheless take the view that frontstage and backstage are not pre-given spaces in the classroom and that what defines frontstage is the combination of the teacher's presence and the students' actions. In short, a static, and exclusively physical distinction between these two different stages does not apply in the classroom because each participant in the classroom decides which actions are public, exposed to the audience consisting of both teacher and all students, and which are more private, only visible to a reduced audience or even no one. Therefore, the notion of back region and front region becomes more dynamic in the classroom setting as it is the students' and lecturer's agencies that shape the different stages.

Elsewhere, Smit (2018) has proposed 'main talk' and 'side talk' to describe the kind of talk that I understand to be constitutive of frontstage and backstage interactions. On the one hand, main talk shapes the frontstage as it involves the lecturer and the whole student group. On the other hand, side talk (either on-topic or off-topic) is often relegated to the backstage because it occurs in parallel to the main classroom activity and it may include just one or a number of students with or without the teacher.

Following Goffman's metaphor of drama, the classroom setting can also be divided into the backstage region and the front region. In the classroom, we can see students' performances, as they selectively display certain behaviour that is expected of them and they tend to follow certain constraints and act appropriately according to the 'unstated' rules of the classroom context. In addition, students' behaviour in the backstage and frontstage often remains different and segregated as the two regions possess 'different accessibility rules and requirements for decorum' (MacCannell, 1990, p. 30). On the one hand, students are in the 'front region' when they participate in class and are engaged in exchanges with the lecturer. They do tasks set by the teacher and use subject-appropriate language while onstage in an EMI class. Their appearance and performance reflects that they are performing 'doing education'. When students engage in non-public side talk amongst themselves during the class, while at the same time the lecturer continues with the main talk and classroom activity and does not pay attention to the students' private interaction, they cross the line into a 'backstage region'. In the backstage of a classroom, students can continue a social interaction with their classmates, as the back region allows 'the loosening of standards' (MacCannell, 1990, p. 30). Therefore, while backstage, students may use the marked language (in an EMI class that would be the L1), they can show a lack of enthusiasm, understanding or knowledge through how they sit or gesture, in ways that would be inappropriate in the front region with the lecturer as the audience.

The comparison of front and backstage behaviour does not imply that one behaviour is more authentic than the other. Students may be dedicated and hard-working or they may complain about the teacher or subject, or they may make jokes about not having studied enough for an exam while engaged in backstage interaction with their classmates. As Meyrowitz (1990, p. 70) explains:

> Nearly everyone exhibits behaviours in one setting that contradict the behaviours they exhibit in other settings. Indeed, even back region behaviour may be thought of as a kind of role, where teammates will not tolerate formal, front region style.

Social interaction therefore involves diverse spaces where individuals perform different roles and adhere to distinct behaviours so as to develop and maintain a specific identity. In this chapter, the aim is to apply Goffman's dramaturgical analysis of social interaction to an interactional episode occurring in an EMI lesson in which – depending on whether they are frontstage or backstage – students act as 'doing education' or 'being a student', respectively (Benwell and Stokoe, 2002). The two spaces of the classroom, the frontstage and the backstage, allow students to subtly negotiate these conflicting identities.

'Being a student' and 'doing education' 47

The 'doing education'/'being a student' dichotomy is adopted from research by Benwell and Stokoe (2002) where they examine university tutorial sessions of both undergraduate and postgraduate students from different disciplines in three British universities. In their work, Benwell and Stokoe found that students may display a reluctance or resistance to show their academic identity. When in class, students both construct and resist their academic identity as they also work to maintain their student identity that they exhibit in social interactions with their classmates. In non-public-turns, students are in the backstage of the classroom setting as they do not orient to the lecturer and they are not engaged in the public forum of the class. In this backstage space, learners do 'being a student': lack of enthusiasm, recognition of lack of knowledge and/or laughter. Onstage, in front of the lecturer as an audience, they may choose to display their academic identity as they are engaged in the business of 'doing education': use of expert language, participation in the interactional dynamic established by the lecturer, and engagement with the task at hand. Although the distinction made by Benwell and Stokoe may not apply to all university contexts, it does resonate strongly with the one examined in this chapter.

This 'being a student'/'doing education' dichotomy is related to both Goffman's concept of 'footing' (1981) and Davies and Harré's (1999) concept of 'positioning' and so they are useful tools to investigate how individuals move and participate in the public and the private domain, that is to say, in frontstage and backstage regions. On the one hand, footing refers to how a participant aligns with co-conversationalists in interactions. As Burns (1992, p. 324) explains:

> the alignment of speaker to audience may change quite frequently and, consequently, has to be repeatedly defined and redefined. Goffman calls this alignment 'footing' and defines it as what occurs 'when as speakers we project ourselves in a current and locally active capacity, then our co-participants in the encounter are the ones who will have their selves partly determined correspondingly.
> (Goffman, 1981, p. 151)

In addition, Burns (1992, p. 325) points out that a change in footing can be marked either by a change in tone or accent, and also it can be indicated through changes in embodiment (posture or gestures). Similar to Goffman's notion of footing is 'positioning', defined by Davies and Harré (1999, p. 37) as 'the discursive process whereby people are located in conversations as observably and subjectively coherent participants in jointly produced storylines'. As Ribeiro (2006, p. 49) points out, the notions of footing and positioning are related but they need to be distinguished as they 'grasp different types of metamessages'. In terms of interactional strategies, footing provides information on participants' subtle shifts in alignment to each other (e.g. from an academic register to a more social and informal register) and positioning informs us about how interaction is oriented and moving into a given direction where positions are negotiated, accepted, and/or refuted. As Ribeiro (2006, p. 74) explains:

> positioning characterizes speaker and hearer's most prominent stances (or projected selves) in interaction, the ones that participants would clearly be identified with or would use to identify the other...[footings] refer to the very micro interactional shifts, which would ultimately constitute positioning. Thus, a shift in pronoun use...and a shift in register...would be a shift in footing but would not necessarily entail a repositioning.

By analysing the positions that students adopt – how they comply, acquiesce, and accept, or how they deny, defy, and resist – we can capture how they present themselves in relation to 'being a student' and 'doing education'. With these concepts in mind, we can view how participants shift from the frontstage to the backstage domain, hence how their footing will move from the institutionalised, official public discourse to a more personal interaction (shift in register) in the private region.

The research

Research participants

In this chapter, I focus on three participants who have been assigned pseudonyms: the lecturer, Isabel, and the students, Genís and Vidal.[2] Isabel is a mechanical engineering lecturer who teaches a BSc-level course on Services II. She is a bilingual speaker of Spanish and Catalan. As an early career academic, Isabel was positively predisposed to EMI. In addition, she claimed to have a C1 English competence and reported a range of international experiences, such as giving papers at conferences, and mobility experiences, such as stays at universities abroad. Isabel revealed a positive view towards Englishisation and seemed to see English as an important and essential element in her academic life: she uses English mainly to write academic articles and to present conference papers and she believes that some disciplinary subjects should be offered in English. Her experience as an English lecturer started out of personal curiosity, it was not a requirement from the university but a voluntary involvement.

Meanwhile, Genís and Vidal are Year 4 students. In terms of English proficiency, Genís has a B1 level in English but Vidal's specific level of English

'Being a student' and 'doing education' 49

is not known, as he did not take the placement test. However, based on my observation of 16 class sessions during the course, I estimate his level to be more or less the same as Genís's, or even a little lower, putting it between an A2 and B1 level. As for their respective participation, Genís often engaged in classroom interaction with the lecturer in English and collaborated with fully constructed English sentences. In contrast, Vidal hardly ever took part in whole-class interactions. In fact, in one audio-recorded episode where Vidal is trying to produce a written answer, he has problems writing the words 'environment' and 'oxygen'.

The data presented in this chapter are taken from the author's in-depth study of a 15-week BSc-level course on services that Isabel taught in English in spring 2018. Over the 15 weeks, there were two class sessions per week, and each session lasted two hours. A total of 12 students (all of them national students, bilingual in Catalan and Spanish) were enrolled in the course – there were no international students in this EMI class. Here, the focus is on one EMI class session that took place in March 2018. The session was about compression refrigeration and was observed and video-recorded with two cameras and recorders placed on students' desks to capture their interactions. The particular excerpt that I examine here has been chosen because of its significance in regard to the research focus and research questions: it has instances of backstage and frontstage multimodal behaviour and it is an example of how students bring different subject positions to the classroom setting, resulting in an ambivalent student identity as it fluctuates between 'doing education' and 'being a student'. In addition, this particular student pair often sat together and they engaged in both on-topic and off-topic interactions. For this reason, I have focused on this student dyad and not others. Ultimately, the extract is in itself an instance of what remains often unnoticed in classroom analysis.

Research methodology

Employing a multimodal analysis methodology, this chapter examines a videotaped interaction between two students and a lecturer in an EMI Engineering class. The use of technologies such as the video has launched the 'video turn' (Mondada, 2019a) in recent years, which allows researchers a more complete view of social life:

> Video recordings allow researchers to observe in repeated and systematic ways…the detailed organization of human action in its social and material context, as it is achieved through the mobilization of coordinated embodied and linguistic resources. Video offers a view on human action that supports its conceptualization as an emergent and temporal phenomenon, situated in its material environment.
>
> (Mondada, 2019a, p. 49)

A key tenet of multimodality is the questioning of the traditional separation of the different meaning-making resources and, in particular, the notion that language is the single most important means through which meaning is conveyed (Crawford Camiciottoli, and Campoy-Cubillo, 2018; Jewit, Bezemer and O'Halloran, 2016; Mondada, 2019b; Norris, 2004). With a multimodal approach, we are taking into account the interplay of the diverse modes: gaze, gestures, facial expressions, body postures, movement, spatial behaviour, speech and prosody, and material objects (Mondada 2018a; Mondada, 2018b, Norris 2004). The acknowledgment that different meaning-making resources may appear in combination with language enables us to approach the interactional episode as a complete whole. By looking at the semiotic resources that emerge during the interactional episode, we can see how the students' identities, both their academic identities (doing education) and their social identities (being a student), emerge, taking into account the multimodal moves that participants bring into the conversation, which also add meaning to the interaction. We thus avoid 'a lingual bias' (Block, 2014). As Block (2014, p. 60) points out: 'individuals are literate across a range of modes, of which language is just one…[and] identity is seen as emergent in the use of a range of semiotic resources in interaction with others'.

The multimodal transcription, following Morell (2018), includes different columns corresponding to different modes at particular times and spatial positions (SP). Hence, there are three columns for three different modes: gaze, gestures/facial expression (divided into two columns, one with the video still and one with a written description), and speech. Therefore, the linguistic repertoire is complemented with the semiotic repertoire, which according to Blackledge and Creese (2017, p. 385) includes '[t]he way people walk, stand, and sit, the way they tilt their head, the gaze of their eyes, the shrug of their shoulders, the movement of their hands and fingers, their smile or frown'. By including 'gaze' in the analysis we can explore the students' 'attention to particular moments' (Cowan, 2014, p. 9), at whom or where students look, for example. Moreover, facial expressions are important because there can be grimaces and winks between students, and gestures are significant in the interactional episode analysis because they accompany speech.

In relation to the presentation of class excerpts (the transcription of talk and multimodal action),[3] there are two sets of transcriptions presented in combination in the form of a table. In one of the columns, I present the simplified set of transcription conventions that I have followed to capture basic essential aspects of spoken language while not impeding readability (found in the sixth column of the tables named as 'Speech'). For reasons of clarity, the multimodal transcription has a total of three columns representing two modes – 'Gaze' and 'Gestures'. The latter has two columns: one where a still of the gesture is provided and a second one where the gesture is explained (if this is necessary). Then, each row represents a proposition of meaning. I have provided two tables (Tables 3.1 and 3.2) for two different moves: the listening move table (Table 3.1), where students are listening to the lecturer's explanation and the peer-scaffolding move table (Table 3.2), where one of the students acts as a mentor. By adding video stills, the transcript 'become[s] much richer…images allow us to perceive details that we cannot easily distinguish in a transcript that only utilizes language' (Norris, 2004, p. 60). Therefore, the multimodal transcription enables the researcher to visualise the ongoing shifts in facial expressions and gestures. Nevertheless, as Norris (2004, p. 65) suggests, the aim is not to analyse the video captures themselves, but 'to use the images to describe the dynamic unfolding of specific moments in time, in which the layout and modes like posture, gesture, and gaze play as much a part as the verbal'.[4]

Analysis

In the following sub-sections, I draw on the Goffmanian concepts of frontstage and backstage as I analyse an extract from the EMI engineering class which has been divided into two parts: (1) the frontstage: listening mode; and (2) the backstage: peer-scaffolding mode. I show how students display both ambivalence towards EMI, as well as a general lack of enthusiasm towards– and an ironic distance from – 'doing education'.

Frontstage: the listening mode

In the frontstage, students are paying attention to the lecturer's explanation and so are processing the new disciplinary content (see Table 3.1). The extract begins with the lecturer (Isabel) trying to elicit an answer from students (SP 1–2). During this time, although Genís changes his seating position (SP 2), his focus does not shift from the lecturer, his gaze is on the lecturer or on the board while he is trying to figure out a response. Eventually, Genís answers the lecturer's question (SP 8) by using a technical word: 'compressor'. Although he does not really engage in the interactional dynamic initiated by the lecturer, he does show his academic identity to the lecturer, and the rest of the class. He does this by providing an answer to the lecturer's question, thus showing that he has been paying attention. Further to this, his contribution to the interaction is a technical term of the discipline.

As Goffman (1959, pp. 15–16) explains, 'when an individual appears in the presence of others, there will usually be some reason for him to mobilize his activity so that it will convey an impression to others which it is in his interest to convey'. Here, Genís seems to be interested in exhibiting

Table 3.1 Front Stage: listening move

Time (min=' sec=")	Spatial position (SP)	Gaze	Gestures	Gestures explained (if necessary)	Speech
00'15"	1	Both on board			
00'57"	2	GEN on board VID on lecturer		GEN changes sitting position	ISA: but physically (.) what does it mean? / (3) X try to connect / those four points / with the equipments / that you have at the left side / (1) and then / you / (1) you (carry) (28)
01'24"	3	GEN on board VID on notes			
01'35"	4	GEN on lecturer VID on board		[GEN shakes his head NO]	ISA: [no idea?] (7)

01'46"	5	Both on lecturer	GEN changes sitting position	ISA: what happens if the / ( ) my evaporator X / let's say (.) forty centimetres okay? / imagine that we have an evaporator like this / (1) and I bring / you know / a new one / with twenty more centimetres (.) / I bring you (.) / sixties (.) / sixty centimetres evaporator / sixty centimetres long evaporator / would you CHANge (1) the forty centimetres one / BY (.) the sixty- centimetres (.) / to improve (.) efficiency or not? (3.) NAN: yes
02'26"	6	Both on lecturer	[GEN grimaces]	ISA: yes (5) who else? (1) yes? no? (4) / [o: imagine] that I bring now (.)
02'38"	7	GEN on lecturer VID on board	[GEN nods]	ISA: I get / em e (.) I'm rich / which. is not true (.) / and I bring you / a very efficient compressor (.) / [okay?] / and a: / and you have here this forty (.) centimetres evaporator /. and a: m:ore efficient compressor (.). / and you have the: / the option of change (.) / one of those things (.) / both of them / or none of them (2)

(Continued)

Table 3.1 Continued

Time (min=' sec=")	Spatial position (SP)	Gaze	Gestures	Gestures explained (if necessary)	Speech
02'53"	8	Both on board			GEN: the compressor ISA: **ja sé que sóc toca collons eh?/. però vull que penseu / va** {I know I'm a pain in the ass eh? / but I want. you to think / come on} (2) compressor
				[GEN nods]	GEN: yes ISA: you would change the [compressor] okay

'Being a student' and 'doing education' 55

Table 3.2 Back Stage: peer-scaffolding move.

Time (min=' sec=")	Spatial position (SP)	Gaze	Gestures	Gestures explained (if necessary)	Speech
03'05"	9	GEN on VID VID on GEN		VID initiates conversation by turning into GEN. GEN turns to VID	VID: no
03'07"	10	GEN on board VID on GEN		GEN shrugs his shoulder and grimaces to express lack of knowledge.	
03'08"	11	Both on board		VID smiles	VID: @
03'15"	12	GEN on board VID on GEN		GEN initiates peer-scaffolding	GEN: **bueno pos sí** {well so I was right} VID: @

(Continued)

Table 3.2 Continued

Time (min=' sec=")	Spatial position (SP)	Gaze	Gestures	Gestures explained (if necessary)	Speech
03'17"	13	GEN on board VID on GEN		GEN pointing to the board.	GEN: **mira / el ú el pots allargar més** {look / number one you can extend it more}
03'19"	14	GEN on VID VID on GEN		VID replies to GEN's explanation.	VID: eh?
03'21"	15	GEN on VID VID On board		GEN points to the board with his index finger	GEN: **el ú / el pots allargar més / llavors** {number one / you can extend it more / then} VID: **però / no un compressors? / no un evaporador** {but / weren't they compressors? / not an evaporator} GEN: **ja / però compressor és per treballar** {right / but the compressor is for working}

'Being a student' and 'doing education' 57

03'24"	16	GEN on VID VID on board		VID nods after GEN's explanation
03'26"	17	VID on GEN GEN on board		VID asks a question	VID: **si (.) si augmenta / l'evaporador X** {if (.) if the evaporator / increases X} GEN: **per continuar l'aigua** {so the water can continue}
03'27"	18	GEN on VID VID on GEN		GEN turns to VID	
03'28"	19	GEN on board VID on GEN		GEN raises his arm and palms up	GEN: **no sé tio /no sé** {I don't. know dude / I don't know} VID: **per això te pregunto / si augmenta l'evaporador augmenta la QA?** {that's why I'm asking / if the evaporator is bigger / the QA increases too?}

Table 3.2 Continued

Time (min=' sec=")	Spatial position (SP)	Gaze	Gestures	Gestures explained (if necessary)	Speech
03'31"	20	GEN on board VID on baord		VID approaches GEN.	
03'32"	21	GEN on board VID on GEN		GEN grimaces "dunno" face and shrugs shoulders.	
03'34'	22	Both on board		VID smiles	
03'58'	23	GEN on lecturer VID on board		GEN addresses ISA	GEN: but / it's better em: / take (.) big things / or big equipment (.) it's better ISA: it's more expensive GEN: **vale** {okay} ISA: the larger it is / the more expensive it would be / but GEN: so / sixty: (.) centimetres evaporator no

his academic identity to demonstrate his expert knowledge. The way he behaves in front of the class and, particularly, in front of the lecturer helps to present himself in a favourable manner in public. He is in control of the impression that he wants to give in this particular situation. The social front of the classroom is 'institutionalized in terms of the abstract stereotyped expectations to which it gives rise, and tends to take on a meaning and stability apart from the specific tasks which happen at the time to be performed in its name' (Goffman, 1959, p. 37). This means that Genís may be taking on the established social roles expected from him because the front is already pre-established before even performing the task and Genís, as a student, may be willing to maintain the expected functioning of the class front: pay attention, respond to lecturer's question, and use academic vocabulary. Therefore, he chooses to display his academic identity.

When Isabel asks: 'no idea?' in SP 4, Genís shows a lack of knowledge as he shakes his head. During SP 5, the lecturer tries to trigger understanding by posing a hypothesis to students. Although Genís still does not seem to know the answer to the lecturer's question, he exhibits engagement in 'doing education' because he is gazing towards the lecturer and tuned in to how she motions to communicate her point during her explanation. Nevertheless, there is a side action in SP 6, a parallel behaviour that is relegated to the backstage region that not even his classmate sitting next to him, Vidal, notices. In this non-public action, Genís shows lack of understanding or knowledge through his facial expression as he grimaces while the lecturer asks: 'who else? yes? no? o: imagine' (SP 6). As the lecturer continues speaking, Genís seems to have understood the disciplinary content as he nods when Isabel asks 'okay?' (SP 7) and then he actually responds in English with a technical term, 'the compressor', followed by Isabel's confirmation check to which Genís answers with a 'yes' (SP 8). In this move, for the most part, Genís shows his academic identity to his audience (the lecturer and the rest of his classmates) as he is the only student who actually replies with expert vocabulary in English. Although his one-word response does not show how much knowledge the student really has, it is a step forward to engage in the interactional classroom dynamic initiated by the lecturer with a content-specific term. Hence, the student is performing as he is expected to, in a classroom setting, when a disciplinary-content question is posed. Although he provides only a single-word answer, he shows the construction of a novice academic identity.

Backstage: the peer-scaffolding mode

The following backstage extract takes place just after the frontstage episode that was analysed above. Now, the lecturer continues lecturing to the whole class while writing on the board; hence, she turns her back to students. In the meantime, Genís and Vidal start a parallel side talk on-topic interaction in their backstage area (see Table 3.2). In backstage, however, the audience for Genís is different: 'by audience segregation the individual ensures that those before whom he plays one of his parts will not be the same individuals before whom he plays a different part in another setting' (Goffman, 1959, p. 57). In this stage, Genís changes his behaviour as his audience now is just his classmate Vidal. In the backstage region, Vidal and Genís are teammates, as Goffman calls it; they share the same role (EMI students) and need to foster the same impression onstage before their audience (lecturer and the other classmates). Vidal and Genís use their backstage region to relax and joke about the event in the front region. While in the frontstage he was 'doing education', now he is 'being a student' (even classmate or friend). In particular, his facial expressions and body gestures change as the 'backstage conduct is one which allows minor acts which might easily be taken as symbolic of intimacy and disrespect for others present and for the region, while front region conduct is one which disallows such potentially offensive behaviour' (Goffman, 1959, p. 129). Genís's behaviour in the backstage would appear inconsistent if it appeared in the frontstage performance, which is why this kind of multimodal interaction is relegated to the backstage due to its more informal nature.

This turn is 'a non-public turn': it is an inaudible murmuring or 'background noise' that cannot be picked up by the camera, as Genís 'does not orient to the tutor or engage in the public forum' (Benwell and Stokoe, 2002, p. 436). Although the camera cannot capture the students' murmuring, the recorder on the table can. Therefore, the combination of the camera and the recorder allow for the combination of linguistic and other semiotic data. The students display gestures and facial expressions that indicate they are unwilling to take part; they show a lack of uptake (SP 10). Genís's behaviour is ambivalent as he both shows participation in the interactional dynamic initiated by the lecturer in the frontstage, but in the backstage, he demonstrates lack of knowledge and understanding. He embodies the 'being a student' identity often associated with laziness, disengagement, and a distancing not only from 'doing education' but also from the lecturer. After having displayed his academic identity, Genís now reclaims his student identity and engages with his classmate, Vidal, through his facial expressions.

We can see a pattern in the way Genís and Vidal behave. Twice during their background peer-scaffolding episode, Vidal asks Genís a question about the topic and twice Genís shrugs or grimaces to show lack of knowledge (SPs 9–10 and SPs 17–21). On both occasions, Vidal smiles after Genís's semiotic cues (SPs 11 and 22). This pattern is relegated to the backstage of the classroom. This kind of behaviour can be associated with the 'being a student' identity; they are constructing a playful context where their social interaction as classmates, and possibly friends, can also take place. Nevertheless, there is an ambivalent co-existence in this space as they also allow it to be a space for peer-scaffolding where Genís acts as a mentor for Vidal, a less competent student (from SP 13 to SP 17). It is interesting to note that Vidal also tries to alternate between 'doing education and 'being a student' considering that he contests Genís's response (SP 15), activating his disciplinary-content knowledge and also his academic identity as Vidal replies to Genís: 'but weren't they compressors? not an evaporator'. Nevertheless, Genís disavows Vidal's answer (also SP 15). Therefore, there is an asymmetry of subject-content knowledge and the students are inhabiting and ascribing expert and non-expert positions through their side-backstage interaction. Genís's mentoring role can be observed when he is explaining and at the same time pointing to the board with his finger (SPs 13 and 15).

As Roth (2001, p. 366) indicates, '[g]estures have both narrative (iconic gesture) and grounding functions (deictic gestures) connecting the gestural and verbal narratives to the pictorial background'. Genís's finger trajectory accompanies their verbal communication and connects it with what the lecturer is writing on the board. In fact, Roth (2001, p. 375) suggests that gestures appear frequently alongside the student's construction of an explanation, thus assisting in their learning. Here I follow Wood, Bruner, and Ross (1976) in their use of scaffolding, drawing on Vygotsky (1978), meaning that language knowledge is constructed through collaborative interactions where participants become active agents in their own learning. In this mentoring episode, in which Genís and Vidal are engaged, one participant acquires the expert or mentor role who helps, assists, and stimulates the less expert and skilful individual. When engaged in peer-scaffolding, one of the students becomes the more skilful individual and there is collaborative interaction between them to solve the disciplinary-content misunderstanding. As Vygotsky puts it:

> the zone of proximal development. It is the distance between the actual developmental level as determined by independent problem solving and the level of potential development as determined through problem solving under adult guidance or in collaboration with more capable peers.
>
> (Vygotsky, 1978, p. 86)

In this excerpt (Table 3.2), we can see how Genís and Vidal engage in dialogue. Vidal seeks Genís's assistance and the latter tries to resolve the problem. This collaboration between the peers suggests that engagement in social dialogue can lead to mediated learning thanks to peer guidance. The ambiguity of this is that while Genís acts as a mentor – that is, as the more competent learner – he, nevertheless, shows through his facial expressions and gestures a lack of knowledge (SPs 10 and 21). What he may be trying to do is 'save face'. Manning (1992) in his study of Goffman (1967) on face-work states that:

> In all social situations, individuals are obliged to project a self that has a 'positive social value'. This image of self is a person's 'face', and we try hard to protect it. There is a general conspiracy to save face so that social situations can also be saved.
> (Manning, 1992, pp. 38–9)

Therefore, Genís has changed footing from speaker to lecturer to speaker to classmate, hence his face-work is now coherent with his new projected self or position, that of student. Therefore, Genís's face-work preserves the 'ritual equilibrium' (Goffman, 1967, p. 45) between both students. In their definition of face, Brown and Levinson (1992, p. 61) refer to the fact that:

> face is something that is emotionally invested, and that can be lost, maintained, or enhanced and must be constantly attended to in interaction...that is to act in ways that assure the other participants that the agent is heedful of the assumptions concerning face.

For this reason, face is understood as 'the public self-image' (Brown and Levinson, 1992, p. 61) that individuals wish to assert. As Manning (1992, pp. 168–9) points out, '[r]itual respect and face-work are interrelated: the former shows regard for others, the latter for self'. That is to say, Genís may be trying to regain a favourable position with Vidal, his classmate and friend, after the public demonstration in the frontstage of his academic identity; hence, he is regaining his student identity. Genís might not wish to appear just as 'doing education', as an expert: he does not want his academic identity to be the only identity present in the classroom setting, in particular with his classmate Vidal. For this reason, Genís also engages in the business of 'being a student' by presenting himself as unknowledgeable and lacking enthusiasm during the social interaction with Vidal. Therefore, 'doing education' and 'being student' are not fully separated but actually integrated in the back region interaction where Genís acts in both manners.

Genís is performing two rituals: one with the lecturer and one with Vidal. As the requirements for each ritual are different, so too are his linguistic and semiotic resources in each social encounter. Genís, hence, unveils a clash of identities in the backstage because he both acquires a peer-scaffolding mentor position, constructing a more authoritative and knowledgeable identity (SPs 13, 15, 17 and 23), and at the same time he shows a disengagement with, or ambivalence towards, the activity set by the lecturer by shrugging and grimacing to suggest lack of knowledge (SPs 10, 19 and 21). Even if there is a paradoxical co-existence of these two positionings, Genís knows with whom and when to sustain each identity because he is following the conventions of each encounter. In fact, the extract finishes with Genís shifting footing from the side backstage talk to the main frontstage talk as he re-engages with the lecturer's explanation, interacting with the lecturer, and giving an answer to the disciplinary-content question posed (SP 23).

Discussion

In the previous section, I focused on, and examined, a classroom interaction divided into two modes: the listening mode and the peer-scaffolding mode. These observations were carried out with a view to seeing how students use linguistic and non-linguistic resources to make sense of the EMI experience. We have therefore managed not only to examine the semiotic resources they use with the lecturer and between peers but also how they construct and fluctuate between their subject positions.

Sometimes we can learn a lot from very little. In line with what Cowan (2014, p. 6) argues:

> [a]lthough such a short episode somewhat limits generalisability, it is hoped that such detailed analysis might generate particular methodological insights regarding transcription of video and the multimodality of naturally occurring interaction, potentially generating theory which could be applied more broadly.

With this episode, we have seen how student identity is displayed through actions such as: (1) reluctance to engage in academic discourse and in the interactional dynamic of the classroom; (2) lack of enthusiasm; (3) laughter and shrugging to distance themselves from 'doing education' and to maintain the social aspects of being students; and (4) silence after long pauses. On the other hand, when students are engaged in doing education, their academic identity appears through the following moves: (1) engagement in academic discourse; (2) use of expert language; (3) answering questions; and (4) helping and clarifying doubts to classmates.

In relation to the first research question – 'what multimodal resources do students use in backstage or frontstage interactions?' – we have seen in this chapter the ways that Genís and Vidal assign certain behaviours (such as grimaces, shrugs, laughter) to the backstage region. Notwithstanding the brevity of the episode, the ethnographic nature of this study enabled the researcher to observe that in the classroom it was typical of students to talk amongst themselves about the content while the lecturer was at the whiteboard writing up and explaining the equations. This fact prompted a closer look into students' side talk and backstage behaviour, and this has resulted in a multimodal analysis uncovering the subtle changes in the students' verbal and embodied actions depending on the stage. This suggests that different multimodal conducts might occur in front and back regions. Nevertheless, there are also multimodal patterns used in the backstage that involve 'doing education', such as the use of hand gestures when Genís and Vidal are independently discussing a doubt between themselves, while the lecturer is simultaneously explaining something to the whole class from the board.

In relation to the second research question – 'the subject positions that students construct' – Genís displays a clash of identities. This clash is perhaps because the classroom offers both a social and an academic space where, as Benwell and Stokoe (2002, p. 446) note:

[b]y delaying knowledge displays and constructing a playful context within which to discuss such information, a framework is created that facilitates students' engagement with the task whilst preserving these ambivalent identities – so although students might be engaged in the business of 'doing education', this cannot be separated from other functions of social interaction.

Both identities are at hand for students and they decide which one takes more prominence depending on the person they are talking to (lecturer or fellow student) and this, in turn, also influences their actions (gestures and facial expressions). Genís shuffles between different selves: the 'being a student' identity clashes with the potential novice 'doing education' identity, the latter being an identity that is still being negotiated and constructed. It seems that Genís aligns with the lecturer's task as he enters the interactional dynamic and actively participates in the resolution of the problem (SP 7–8 and 23). There is an extended IRF sequence initiated by the lecturer. This is followed by Genís's minimal response and the subsequent lecturer's evaluation and feedback to all students from the board. Although the lecturer does almost all the talking from the board as she explains her point to the whole class, both lecturer and student are 'demonstrating alignment in their orientation to the task at hand' (Tadic, 2016, p. 46). This is because, on the surface, Genís seems to be engaged not only in the IRF sequence but also with the academic content. Immediately after this, it is clear, however, that Genís, in fact, does not show a positive stance towards the task. His action reveals a misalignment due to his embodied conduct in the backstage. In the backstage, we can see Genís's attitude towards the resolution of the problem more explicitly through his facial expression and body movements. His embodied disengagement (SPs 10 and 21) and verbal displays (SPs 19) signal a negative stance towards exhibiting his academic identity and ambivalence with the demonstration of disciplinary knowledge after the content-question posed by the lecturer. He has shifted his stance from an academic position that shows engagement to a student position that portrays disengagement and lack of enthusiasm and knowledge. This shift in his position only becomes clear through his embodied cues that signal a lack of understanding.

Ultimately, students may arrive at conceptual understandings during a peer-scaffolding episode occurring in the backstage region. We have seen how these students' approaches to tasks contribute to an 'interactional framework' in which Genís emerges and self-positions as the leading expert. According to Borràs and Moore (2019, p. 107), 'linguistic expertise also influences the perception that co-participants have of their subject matter expertise'. Therefore, Genís's relatively higher competence in English (as noted above in the 'Research Participants' section) also contributes to him being positioned as expert in the academic content as well. This occurs not only because of his one-word response (SP 8), but also because of the English interaction with the lecturer at the end of the extract (SP 23). Meanwhile, Vidal tries to mobilise his own subject matter knowledge and contest Genís's expert position and challenge his own non-expert identity, which has been attributed to him as Genís inhabits the mentor identity.

There are clear learning implications for the emerging positions of students as experts and non-experts as Vidal is the one who asks and Genís the one who explains ('self-initiated' in contrast to 'other-initiated', and 'self-repair' in contrast to 'other-repair'). Promoting pair-work or group-work activities is advised, especially in EMI lectures where students may be more reluctant to ask and participate in class (Airey and Linder, 2006). Accordingly, this tandem of expert and non-expert student dyad allows students to display, self-inhabit, and other-ascribe expert and non-expert positionings as these interactions may lead to negotiations on the meaning of disciplinary content between students.

Following Benwell and Stokoe (2002), the multimodal analysis undertaken in this chapter reveals that students' use of semiotic resources influence, and may even determine, the subject position adopted and constructed. As we have seen, each mode realises different functions. Thus, while Genís's shrugging and grimacing suggest a 'being a student' position, the movement of his hands and fingers when explaining the equation from the board reveals a 'doing education' position. In this interactive classroom episode, the students' multimodal ensembles explored have revealed the hidden and undisclosed linguistic and embodied actions of EMI students in a higher education context. This has been achieved by examining the issue of how students may display ambivalence towards EMI, as well as a likely general lack of enthusiasm towards – and an ironic distance from – 'doing education'. This lack of enthusiasm, which could also be referred to as a sign of indifference or a careless attitude, is determined by Genís's firmer grasp of the new knowledge in comparison to Vidal, even if it is not firm enough, as he cannot fully answer Vidal's question.

In my view, the 'secret life of EMI' and, in particular, that of at least two EMI students, has been revealed through a multimodal analysis: not only their use of L1 and their shuffling between different positions, but also their use of situated multimodal ensembles. Although the shifts in Genís's footing, from an open-public engagement with the lecturer mainly in English to a private engagement with his peer Vidal, are typical student behaviour of any classroom, both the frontstage/backstage (or main talk/side talk) perspective and the multimodal analysis have uncovered an often under-research but intriguing area: students' private interaction in all its modes. The multimodal analysis advances our understanding of what goes on specifically in an EMI classroom: students' low participation seems to be compensated through student-student interactions. Instead of taking advantage of the lecturer's expert knowledge and engaging in interaction with her, learners in these student-dyads negotiate both their emergent content-expert and language-expert positions through peer-scaffolding to process and develop their disciplinary knowledge. This analysis thus enables us to uncover the different positions constructed by students in a classroom setting – positionings which could only be discovered by taking into account the whole 'orchestration of modes' (Morell, 2018, p. 77).

In conclusion, this chapter provides much food for thought on how EMI unfolds in classroom practices. In the scenario examined here, even though this is an EMI class, students' behaviour would probably be similar in an L1-medium of instruction class. There is a minimum amount of English being used and when it is used it is in a teacher-student dyad. Seldom do learners use English under a student-student tandem, unless it is to refer to specific lexical items such as 'compressors'. Given this state of affairs, it can be observed that students are not reasoning academically in English, so there is no real deeper reasoning going on in the L2, which presumably is an important aim of EMI. There is, however, student-student dyad peer-scaffolding and (possibly) learning occurring in Catalan, which raises the question of what purpose EMI serves here. If EMI is implemented following an explicit internationalisation objective to attract international students and this aim is not met, the result is an EMI class with a homogenous group of local students who share the same L1 with the lecturer. Therefore, in a way, EMI is theatricalised because neither the explicit internationalisation objective is accomplished, nor the implicit language-learning objective is enforced. For this reason, we are left to consider that this class could have been executed equally – or even more – successfully if they had switched back to L1-content teaching. Further to this, and in terms of research methodology, this analysis has also shown that without a camera we could have only seen Genís's academic identity and his engagement in doing education through the audio recording. The video recording, however, has allowed us to analyse his multimodal cues, revealing the limitation of using solely audio recordings to analyse classroom-situated events and phenomena.

Notes

1. All data cited in this chapter is from the project *Towards an empirical assessment of the impact of English medium instruction at university: language learning, disciplinary knowledge and academic identities* (ASSEMID), funded by the Spanish Ministry of Economy, Industry and Competitiveness (*El Ministerio de Economía, Industria y Competitividad* – MINECO), code FFI2016-76383-P. 30 December 2016 – 29 December 2019.
2. All names have been anonymised.
3. All excerpts have been transcribed using the following conventions:

Convention	Function
/	Indicates natural pauses between units of speech.
...	Text edited out (e.g. hesitations, false starts, pauses of one second or more, incomprehensible speech).
bold	In the class excerpts, anything not said in English is marked in bold.
{ }	English translations of classroom speech in Catalan are provided in curly brackets.
Capital letters	Words uttered with emphasis.
[ ]	Overlapping. Whenever utterances and gestures happen at the same time, the overlaps are marked with squared brackets.
?	Rising intonation (as in a question).
X	Unintelligible speech.
(.)	Every brief pause in speech (up to a good half second) is marked with a full stop in parentheses.
(1)	Longer pauses are timed to the nearest second and marked with the number of seconds in parentheses, e.g. (1) = 1 second, (3) = 3 seconds.
:	Lengthened sounds are marked with a colon.
@	All laughter and laughter-like sounds are transcribed with the @ symbol.

4. It should be noted that both students gave permission for their images to be reproduced without blurring.

References

Airey, J., & Linder, C. (2006). Language and the experience of learning university physics in Sweden. *European Journal of Physics, 27*(3), 553–560.

Benwell, B. M., & Stokoe, E. M. (2002). Constructing discussion tasks in university tutorials: Shifting dynamics and identities. *Discourse Studies, 4*(4), 429–453.

Blackledge, A., & Creese, A. (2017). Translanguaging and the body. *International Journal of Multilingualism, 14*(3), 250–268.

Block, D. (2014). Moving beyond 'lingualism': Multilingual embodiment and multimodality in SLA. In S. May (Ed.), *The multilingual turn: Implications for SLA, TESOL and bilingual education* (pp. 54–77). London: Routledge.

Borràs, E., & Moore, E. (2019). The plurilingual and multimodal management of participation and subject complexity in university CLIL teamwork. *English Language Teaching, 12*(2), 100–112.

Brown, P., & Levinson, S. C. (1992). *Politeness: Some universals in language usage*. Cambridge: Cambridge University Press.

Burns, T. (1992). *Erving Goffman*. London: Routledge.

Cowan, K. (2014). Multimodal transcription of video: Examining interaction in early years classrooms. *Classroom Discourse, 5*(1), 6–21.

Crawford Camiciottoli, B., & Campoy-Cubillo, M. C. (2018). Introduction: The nexus of multimodality, multimodal literacy, and English language teaching in research and practice in higher education settings. *System, 77*(1), 1–9.

Davies, B., & Harré, R. (1999). Positioning: The discursive production of selves. *Journal for the Theory of Social Behaviour, 20*(1), 43–63.

Goffman, E. (1959). *The presentation of self in everyday life*. London: Penguin.

Goffman, E. (1967). *Interaction ritual: Essays on face-to-face behaviour*. New York, NY: Pantheon Books.

Goffman, E. (1981). *Forms of talk*. Oxford: Blackwell Publishing.

Jewit, C., Bezemer, J., & O'Halloran, K. (2016). *Introducing multimodality*. London: Routledge.

MacCannell, D. (1990). The descent of the ego. In S. H. Riggins (Ed.), *Beyond Goffman: Studies on communication, institution, and social interaction* (pp. 19–40). New York, NY: Mouton de Gruyter.

Manning, P. (1992). *Erving Goffman and modern sociology*. Cambridge: Polity Press.

Meyrowitz, J. (1990). Redefining the situation: Extending dramaturgy into a theory of social change and media effect. In S. H. Riggins (Ed.), *Beyond Goffman: Studies on communication, institution, and social interaction* (pp. 65–98). New York, NY: Mouton de Gruyter.

Mondada, L. (2018a). Greetings as a device to find out and establish the language of service encounters in multilingual settings. *Journal of Pragmatics, 126*, 10–28.

Mondada, L. (2018b). Multiple temporalities of language and body in interaction: Challenges for transcribing multimodality. *Research on Language and Social Interaction, 51*(1), 85–106.

Mondada, L. (2019a). Contemporary issues in conversation analysis: Embodiment and materiality, multimodality and multisensoriality in social interaction. *Journal of Pragmatics, 145*, 47–62.

Mondada, L. (2019b). Transcribing silent actions: A multimodal approach of sequence organization. *Social Interaction. Video-Based Studies of Human Sociality*, *2*(1). doi:10.7146/si.v2i1.113150.

Morell, T. (2018). Multimodal competence and effective interactive lecturing. *System*, *77*(1), 70–79.

Norris, S. (2004). *Analyzing multimodal interaction: A methodological framework*. New York, NY: Routledge.

Ribeiro, B. T. (2006). Footing, positioning, voice. Are we talking about the same things? In A. De Fina, D. Schiffrin & M. Bamberg (Eds.), *Discourse and identity* (pp. 48–82). Cambridge: Cambridge University Press.

Robinson, L., & Schulz, J. (2016). Eliciting frontstage and backstage talk with the iterated questioning approach. *Sociological Methodology*, *46*(1), 53–83.

Roth, W. (2001). Gestures: Their role in teaching and learning. *Review of Educational Research*, *7*(3), 365–392.

Smit, U. (2018). Classroom discourse in EMI. On the dynamics of multilingual practices. In K. Murata (Ed.), *English-medium instruction from an English as a Lingua Franca Perspective* (pp. 99–117). London: Routledge.

Tadic, N. (2016). Signaling learner stance through multimodal resources. *Working Papers in TESOL & Applied Linguistics*, *16*(2), 44–50.

Thornborrow, J., & Haarman, L. (2012). Backstage activities as frontstage news. *European Journal of Communication*, *27*(4), 376–394.

Vygotsky, L. S. (1978). *Mind in society: The development of higher psychological processes*. London: Harvard University Press.

Wood, D., Bruner, J. S., & Ross, G. (1976). The role of tutoring in problem solving. *Journal of Child Psychology and Psychiatry*, *17*(2), 89–100.

4 Whispers of resistance to EMI policies

The management of Englishisation through alternative local multilingual practices and dissenting identities[1]

Maria Sabaté-Dalmau

Introduction: language-in-education policies, Englishisation, and EMI

Under the conditions of the globalised new economy, universities have turned into profit-making educational systems which follow the logics of 'educational neoliberalism' (Block, 2018), here understood as a form of institutional governance and as a rationality/ideology (Martín Rojo, 2019).

In the Catalan tertiary education system, these 'market adjustments' (Söderlundh, 2012, p. 89) have resulted in a series of 'multilingualisation' missions aimed at market expansion based on the incorporation of 'productive' global languages, along with local/minority languages, in the curriculum, as a way to internationalise it (Llurda et al., 2015). As in most non-English-speaking universities (see Mortensen, 2014), in Catalonia multilingualisation policies have been implemented through the officialisation of English as 'the preferred language choice' (Secretariat for Universities and Research, 2015), in 'English-plus-local-languages' policy configurations that envision the 'commonsensical' efficient management of linguistic diversity in/through this 'politically-neutral' lingua franca which has come to index 'innovation', 'leadership', and 'professionalism' (Sabaté-Dalmau, 2016). These positive orientations towards English are in line with neoliberal 'resource-rationalisation/efficiency' logics which justify the 'obvious' choice of English by constructing it as an international 'academic asset' and 'employability requirement' in the new economic order (Mortensen and Haberland, 2012; Piller and Cho, 2013).

Following suit, many Englishisation plans in Catalonia have been undertaken which aim at 'skilling' educational agents in English, under the assumption that the use of this language is scarce in this institutional domain

(Armengol et al.; 2013; Bretxa, Comajoan and Vila, 2016). One such plan is the relatively recent but quick introduction of EMI, implemented in different ways in multilingual universities across Europe (Söderlundh, 2012). In the context analysed, EMI has been operationalised in a largely unstructured, unplanned manner (Block and Khan, this volume), with a lack of institutional support and training for educational agents (Mancho-Barés and Arnó-Macià, 2017). Despite this, it has been eagerly embraced as a niche of 'excellence' and 'distinction'. For educational agents, it has become an index of prestige, as those who engage in it are considered 'more qualified' and professionally 'worthier' than 'ordinary' lecturers who teach in local languages (Dafouz, 2018).

My objective in this chapter is to contribute to the body of research which analyses the interplay between global Englishisation reforms and local 'top-down' policies by trying to understand what these entail for educational agents. These agents are required to implement EMI, developing alternative practice-based language policies 'from below' which involve the 'supplementary' use of local language(s) (see, e.g., Hazel and Mortensen, 2013; Söderlundh, 2013) in non-English-speaking Southern European universities (see, e.g., Cots, 2013). Departing from the problematisation of current language-in-education policies, the specific aim is to contribute to the exploration of discrepancies and incongruities in situated language practices in an EMI class which contravene English-only rules in one bilingual European university with a majority and a minority language; in this case, respectively, Spanish and Catalan.[2] By focusing on EMI lecturers and students' interactions, I expand the research scope of the above-referenced sociolinguistic studies which provide a socio-politically grounded view of the quandaries of EMI pedagogies. Of particular interest are the social meanings of 'bottom-up' contradictions, clashes, and subversive acts that emerge when newer Englishisation policies are taken up and 'navigated', on the ground, in a non-normative manner by 'non-native' EMI lecturers, and students in routine classroom interactions. To this end, I propose an interpretive framework and reflexive research tool to investigate the interactional microphenomena, metaphorically called 'whispers of resistance', whereby these two groups of educational agents show resistance to supranational and local English-language regimes which are difficult to document and to theorise. In what follows, I provide the details of this proposal as well as the conceptual underpinnings that informed this study.

Aims and theoretical considerations

From a *critical ethnographic sociolinguistics* approach to language in institutions (Duchêne, Moyer and Roberts, 2013), in this chapter I provide an account of 'bottom-up' sociolinguistic behaviours mobilised by educational agents which are revealing of oppositional orientations towards global language-in-education projects and local English-language normativities. More specifically, I try to answers the following six questions concerning the reasons why EMI lecturers and students show resistance or distancing from English-only directives without compromising the Englishisation mission:

- How: with which language practices and academic identities?
- To what extent: on which occasions? In which classroom events?
- When: in public- and/or private-performance time?
- Where: in which zones of the institutional setting?
- Why: for which personal, academic/professional purposes? and
- With what consequences: with which resulting language ecologies?

In order to establish a disciplined way to investigate the social meanings of these subversive breaches of English-language norms, I propose the concept 'whispers of resistance'. I understand it as a working theoretical framework and as an exploratory tool to try to provide clarity to what we mean by situated (and underreported) bottom-up 'resistance actions' that, from a socially-engaged perspective, shall be 'the subject of pedagogical considerations' (Giroux, 1983, p. 291) for assessing EMI strategies and for advancing in the design of effective EMI pedagogies. I narrow down 'whispers of resistance' to the analysis of local language use and of plurilingual English; that is, non-standard forms of English which bear traces of individuals' multilingual resources (Moore, Borràs and Nussbaum, 2013).

The framework proposed is grounded upon four main theoretical underpinnings, summarised as follows. Firstly, I take the political economic perspective developed by Flubacher, Duchêne and Coray (2018) and I apply it to Englishisation reforms which understand neoliberal language policies and historicised and contextualised practices in HE classrooms as dialogically intertwined. That is, I follow the view that given language directives are socio-political actions (Codó, 2018) whose objective is to redress particular local interactional dynamics; and that classroom practices are reflective of how policies are managed in daily communication, here in EMI.

Secondly, I understand ambivalent, contradictory and/or negative orientations towards Englishisation and EMI as indexes of observable sociolinguistic norms and rationalities which govern individual/collective language comportments under the conditions of market-oriented educational neoliberalism.

Thirdly, I approach the English-mediated identity practices which emanate from these shifting perspectives as a lens into how individuals develop, negotiate, assert and/or reject who they are, when they provide accounts for their language-based subject positionings by presenting themselves (and others) with particular academic ethos (Martín Rojo, 2019). My starting point is Moncada-Comas and Block's (2019) model that analysed EMI lecturers' and students' academic identity acts, which they, in turn, based on the model proposed by Benwell and Stokoe (2002) for the analysis of 'resistant or distancing' identity behaviours in HE (Benwell and Stokoe, 2005, p. 139). I adapt Moncada-Comas and Block's (2019) framework to locate educational agents' identity displays along two axes of a 'resistant/compliant identity' continuum. On the one end of this continuum, I locate the instances of resistant identities of individuals who take up roles as 'being a student'/'content transmitter' that involve displaying 'ambivalence, lack of enthusiasm and…distance from HE culture' (Benwell and Stokoe, 2002, p. 446), showing disengagement with normative English-language rules in class. On the other end of the spectrum, I locate instances of compliant academic identities concerning the 'doing education' (Benwell and Stokoe, 2002, p. 446), which involves using 'expert' language and properly accomplishing the teacher/student lecturing tasks required in EMI.

I focus on EMI lecturers and students because they are crucial agents for the success or failure of language policy implementation (Lasagabaster, Cots and Mancho-Barés, 2013). I believe that the important personal changes which they experience in terms of academic/professional development when they start to teach or to be instructed in an FL are turning points in life which lead them to reshape their orientations towards languages, to adapt their sociolinguistic comportments, and to renegotiate their language-based personhoods (Pujolar, 2019); for example, by presenting themselves as (non)-proficient EFL users. In this regard, I draw on the 'multilingual individual' as the locus for unpacking the ways in which language policies are understood, adopted, challenged, or resisted in interpersonal communication (Spolsky, 2019); in this case, under neoliberal frames of reference which require educational agents to behave as self-managed, disciplined, rational personas (Sabaté-Dalmau, 2020). This justifies my decision to conduct an in-depth micro interactional analysis on instances of whispers of resistance in a single EMI class, studying EMI lecturers and students on a case-study basis.

Fourthly, I draw on my own notion of resistance (Sabaté i Dalmau, 2014) to conceptualise 'whispers of resistance' as implicit (sub)conscious oppositional practices emerging 'from below' that contradict and disrupt top-down English-language policies, *without* jeopardising them. That is, I understand acts of resistance as *non-accidental* subversive breaches of the norms which display a certain degree of individual/collective empowerment to skirt language policies and to operate through alternative multilingual local-language classroom rules which challenge but which do not ultimately galvanise English-only regimes. In this regard, I follow the view that these confronting 'counter-conducts or conducts done differently...with other procedures/methods' (Martín Rojo, 2019, p. 184) co-occur with, and emerge in connection to, acts of compliance to Englishisation norms that get mobilised along with them, in the same EMI class, by the same educational agents. This perspective allows us to unpack how educational agents manage the contradictions and tensions which emerge when global English-language policies are implemented in institutions whose local routine classroom dynamics are *de facto* multilingual (Mortensen, 2014; Söderlundh, 2012, 2013).

'Whispers' are 'quiet' yet audible soft sounds and hushed, though buzzing, interactional acts that are meant to be private. They interfere in, and disrupt, the communicative events in which they are mobilised, without compromising them. I employ the term 'whispers of resistance' (rather than 'resistance') because this allows me to better capture the complex nature of intrusive, deviant EMI practices which pose a challenge to the Englishisation project but which, in effect, make it operational, naturalising its neoliberal workings and ideological underpinnings. The use of 'whispers' also allows me to unpack contravening identities which show an opposition to the demands requiring university agents to become efficient (nativelike) academic English users but which in fact reveal an individual/collective investment in 'self-Englishisation'.

In order to offer a comprehensive rationale of observed whispers of resistance which integrates interplaying compliance acts, I draw on Goffman's (1959) model for the provision of micro-accounts of routine interactions, here adapted to the analysis of EMI practices and identities, as shown in Figure 4.1.

Employing Goffman's seminal theatrical metaphors, I address *frontstage* behaviours as theoretically 'public' sociolinguistic comportments that display compliance to EMI rules, as they reveal how educational agents follow established monoglossic English-only normativities, leaving the Englishisation plans which they are required to operationalise unquestioned. I link these legitimate behaviours, also conceptualised as institutional 'on-task' talk (Söderlundh, 2013, p. 90), to the ways in which EMI lecturers and students invest in presentations of the self as individuals properly 'doing education'. This allows them to mobilise successful neoliberal educational ethos as proficient 'self-Englishised' educational agents.

I understand *backstage* behaviours as theoretically 'private' comportments that display resistance to EMI, observed when educational agents, taking up self-responsible 'being a student'–'content transmitter' roles, unconsciously *and* consciously make use of local languages and of plurilingual English, in the oral and written modes. This backstage talk, also

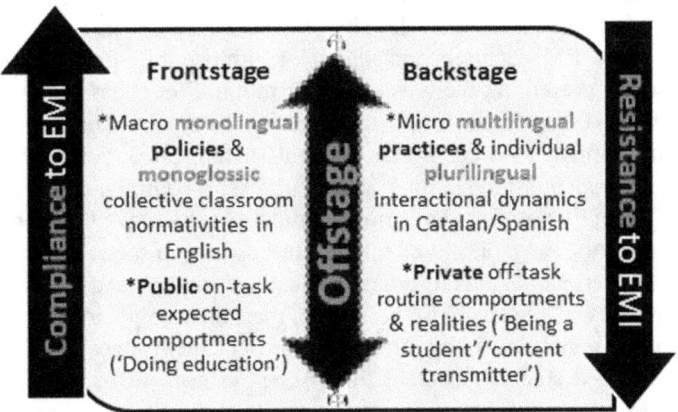

Figure 4.1 A Goffman-inspired framework for the analysis of 'whispers of resistance'.

approached as non-institutional 'off-task' talk (Söderlundh, 2013, p. 90), in effect contradicts the very nature of the EMI project and may show us under what conditions instruction in English 'fails' in terms of 'pragmatic' communicative effectiveness.

I approach front- and backstage behaviours as standing in a dialogic relationship along a *frontstage-compliance* and *backstage-resistance* spectrum. This allows me to highlight the centrality of the 'fuzzy' and 'porous' interactional space of 'offstage' performance, where EMI actors ideologically frame most of their counter-comportments (this is marked as a double-headed arrow delineated by a broken line in the centre of the framework in Figure 4.1). 'Offstage' practices emerge at the crossroads of front- and backstage spaces (Rose, Diamond and Baker, 2010), because they are visible and occur in public, but in less-disruptive 'interlude' transition times (e.g. during breaks or right before/after class), and in 'darkened' zones of the classroom 'stage' (the corridor, the instructor's table). I understand them as 'liminal institutional interactions' (Hazel and Mortensen, 2013, p. 3) which are neither totally formalised nor explicitly legitimised by educational agents, since they occur when the classroom 'stage' (and its educational agents' comportments) is not 'illuminated'. In other words, offstage performance is deviating performance which is acknowledged but which is presented as 'side talk' (Söderlundh, 2012, p.

97) that is not constitutive of the expected homogeneous English 'floor' in EMI.

Offstage interactions also fuse the boundaries between compliant-identity ('doing education') acts and resistance-identity ('being a student'/'content-transmitter') presentations of the self. This is so because offstage performance reveals how EMI lecturers and students legitimise their on-/off-talk resistance acts by presenting them as syncretic routine 'let-it-pass' strategies (Firth, 1996). These do not follow the rules but are rendered necessary and are 'made normal' (Moore, Borràs and Nussbaum, 2013, p. 67), for efficient content transmission/learning, when successful communication in EFL is perceived to be at risk. The normalisation of subversive comportments as a transitory 'way-out' to effectively teach/learn in the EMI class allows these educational agents to provide a justification for, and to grant linguistic 'authority' (Preisler, 2014, p. 218) to, their disengaged identities. This is a Goffmanian face-saving strategy to present themselves as self-responsible 'being a student'/'content transmitter' in need to be resolute when 'coming to the point' in class – that is, to claim legitimacy as proficient EMI interactants through 'resistant-yet-compliant' multilingual ethos.

Overall, the Goffman-inspired model proposed here, by situating resistance and compliance acts along a markedly fluid, complex spectrum, allows for the contextualisation of whispers of resistance as occurring in an institutional setting (a classroom with scarce 'darkened' room for intimate talk) where educational agents closely self-monitor and modulate academic performance with a high degree of self-reflexivity. It thereby allows us to shed new light on the extent to which 'non-authenticated' behaviour is modulated through the agents' perceived 'degree of institutionality of particular interactional situations' (Söderlundh, 2013, p. 90) in a formal 'stage' which is hierarchically regimented in terms of language choices/uses and of the distribution and organisation of student/teacher talking-time and turn-taking (Benwell and Stokoe, 2002).

The context: setting, methods, data, and participants

The EMI course 'Animal health and production'

I apply the discussed framework to my monitoring of a 4th-year elective course in the Biotechnology Degree which took place during the first term of the academic year 2017/18, and which involved two EMI lecturers and 25 final-year students. It was to be conducted only in English, as explained by the instructor, Anna (pseudonym):[3]

> The English courses shall be all in English -, you can't simply have the PowerPoint in English and then <expl> [//] > explain in <Catal>

[//] and in <Span>,, <ok> [?]. This is what the Director of Studies has told us.[4]

(interview; 5 October 2017)

The observed course module consisted of 12 two-hour sessions of formal lecturing (18 hours) and practical fieldwork activities in a laboratory, a goat farm, and a research centre.

In terms of curriculum, the course had two main aims, presented in a separate manner (see Figure 4.2): one was about 'science' (providing an introduction to 'Animal health'); and the other one about 'language' (providing tools for EFL improvement). Its specific objectives in terms of content were to get students familiarised with the theoretical and methodological principles and work dynamics, of the following activities: Intensive/extensive farming; dairy cattle management; health intervention techniques for ovine, caprine, and beef cattle; swine production; and common treatments for animal-infectious diseases. In terms of language, it was assumed that the lecturer would have a (CEFR) C1-level of English so as to transmit disciplinary knowledge in it, and that students would depart from a B2 level of competence that would be the basis to expand their proficiency in four EFL 'skills' (listed in Figure 4.2). Thus, EMI in this class was grounded on a simplistic view of FL improvement as occurring 'naturally' in an immersive manner, by virtue of exposing students to it.

The methodology employed for formal lecturing was based on flipped learning (see Prieto Martín, 2017): Students accessed the materials (handouts and PowerPoints) 24 hours before each session, and the lecturer used the class time not only to ensure that the content provided in the materials had been transmitted but also to further their understanding through discussion tasks. The assessment for this first part (accounting for 50% of the final

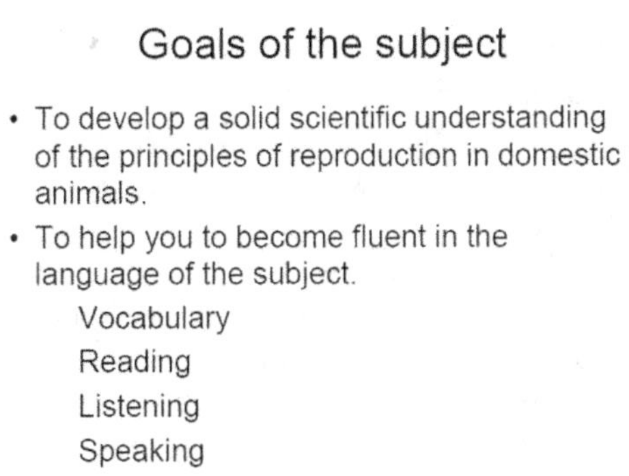

Goals of the subject

- To develop a solid scientific understanding of the principles of reproduction in domestic animals.
- To help you to become fluent in the language of the subject.
    Vocabulary
    Reading
    Listening
    Speaking

Figure 4.2 Course Objectives. Introductory PowerPoint slide (9/1/18).

grades of the course) consisted of an exam (30%); out-of-class tasks (13%); and in-class exercises (7%).

Methods and data

The data concerning the course was collected within the ASSEMID project, from which I selected the following sets:

1) Two audio-recorded semi-structured interviews with the lecturer, Anna. These were conducted in the language of her choice, Catalan, and were transcribed verbatim (see transcription system in Appendix 1). The first (pre-observation) interview lasted for an hour and 28 minutes. It concerned the following aspects of her background up to the time of the study: academic life, research trajectory as well as career accomplishments; mobility experiences, language background, and multilingual competence involving English. The second (post-observation) interview lasted for an hour and a half and addressed her perceptions concerning her observed EMI performance and her plans for conducting more/fewer EMI courses in the future. I established rapport with Anna prior to observation; contact and visits continue at the time of writing.

2) Video- and audio-recorded classroom interactions were collected every two weeks. These lasted a total of 11 hours and 52 minutes and gathered educational agents' non-linguistic comportments. The classroom layout for the collection of this dataset, handwritten by the researcher as she observed the class, is presented in Figure 4.3. In this layout, Anna's usual teacher-fronted position (behind the board and the screen) is circled in red, which also indicates the location of her microphone. The seven student groups under analysis are circled in black, with the position of the ten audio-recorders employed to gather teacher-student and peer-to-peer occurrences indicated with numbers. The location of the two cameras in the room is indicated with camera icons (the one at the top provided the students' frontal view; and the one at the bottom, which allowed for the observation of students' rear view, was directed towards Anna).

3) 79 student and 11 lecturer audio logs were sent to the researcher via WhatsApp, upon completion of each class. These mobile-phone mediated logs (personal 'reports') were participants' responses to a rubric composed of questions about the following aspects of each session: disciplinary knowledge transmission/learning; multilingual dynamics and English-language teaching/learning events; teacher/students' questions on content/language; perception of teacher/

"Animal Health and Production": Classroom layout

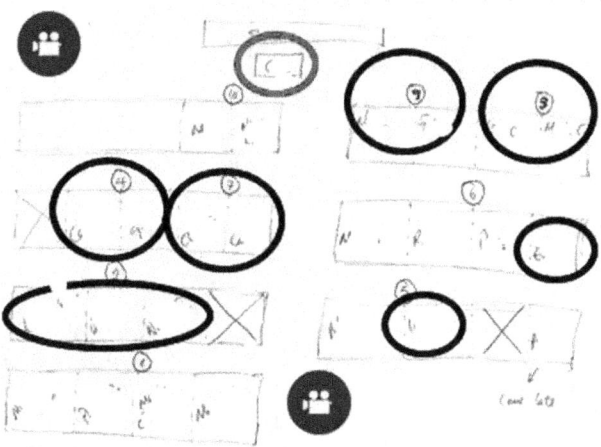

Figure 4.3 Classroom lay-out for data collection.

students' attitudes/practices; and perceptions on one's individual performance.
4) A pre-observation English-language placement test (based on UCLES, 2001) and a background information questionnaire completed online by students. The latter gathered information on their linguistic, mobility, and academic trajectories, their course expectations and professional prospects, as well as their self-reported level of proficiency in four EFL 'skills'.
5) Classroom materials including study notes, PowerPoints, and exams.

Participants' profiles

Anna completed her PhD in 1988, at the University of Santiago de Compostela. Prior to that, she had studied Veterinary Sciences at the University of Zaragoza and had held a pre-doctoral position at the University of León. During this time, she also conducted research in the US. She had been a self-employed entrepreneur for a well-known Spanish agrofood firm and had been hired by the Catalan Ministry of Agriculture for over 16 years. She started working as a part-time lecturer at UdL in 2005, where she got a permanent position as associate professor in 2008.

Anna was a Catalan and Spanish 'native' speaker with the equivalent of a C2-level of English. She also had knowledge of Galician, French, German, Portuguese, and Arabic. She engaged in EMI in 2011–12, when, upon request by the Head of the Department, she self-selected to start deploying it – as she phrased it, 'I volunteered'[5] (interview; 5 October 2017). In 2012–13, she enrolled in the UdL CLIL courses and, since then, she has been teaching two EMI subjects, together with two other lecturers who also lead the implementation of EMI in Animal Sciences.

Anna showed a positive orientation towards the internationalising English-language policies at UdL. She followed the outcomes-oriented economic view of languages, which understands English as a profitable academic 'skill' and employability tool. This is seen in her statement:

> I think they [students] need to know a terminology <of course> [!] because later it'd all sound Chinese. [...] If [you] want to search information if you do this the search in Catalan and in Spanish is very # scarce. [...] Now a biotechnologist [...] the research that they do shall be in English [...] companies <man> [//] managing animal production -, or animal health.[6]
>
> (interview; 5 October 2017)

With this, Anna constructed the non-command of basic English terminology as non-communication (with 'it'd all sound Chinese'), and she categorised the command of work-related knowledge in local languages as 'not enough' for career development; in fact, as a hindrance to access up-to-date information, linking the use of Catalan/Spanish to non-efficiency, and lack of innovation in academia and at the workplace.

In terms of academic identity, she described her English as 'Catalan English';[7] that is, as an 'accented' plurilingual local English which aims at, but does not meet, the standard 'native' English speaker norms. Aligning herself with 'content transmitter' identities, she claimed linguistic authority (i.e., she justified her non-standard English practices) by presenting herself as a specialist lecturer, rather than as an EFL teacher (for similar findings, see Mancho-Barés and Arnó-Macià, 2017), with comments like 'I do not command English enough so as to correct a student'[8] (interview; 5 October 2017) – in fact, the only 'language' assessment that she conducted was a 'glossary' provided by students which included 89 English-to-Spanish/Catalan translations and definitions of particular terminology.

The 25 students' profiles were as follows: twenty of them were female and five were male. All but three (who were repeating students) had started Biotechnology in 2014–15, and they had a mean age of 21 years and five months. Two of them held Colombian nationality, and the rest were Spanish nationals. Five of them had both Catalan and Spanish as their L1; 11 had Spanish as their L1; and five had Catalan. Four students left this question unanswered.

The placement test indicated that they had an average B1-level of English, despite the fact that in their background questionnaire they self-reported having, on average, a B2-level of English, with most self-attributed proficiency in 'reading' and least self-attributed proficiency in 'speaking'. They had been deeply invested in EFL throughout their high-school education. Two held a C1-level of English; 12 held B2-level; and two held the B1-level certificate. 17 had participated in high school student exchanges, in the US, the UK, Ireland, Germany, and the Netherlands. Notably, before beginning university, one of them had participated in a CLIL 'Science' course (part of the government's 'Active Language Learning Plan'); and one had participated in an International Science Camp in Germany.

At the time of the research, 14 students were attending English classes in language schools or through private lessons. Two had been on Erasmus stays (in Norway and Belgium) and three had shared a flat abroad with international students. Another two had conducted their practicum in an English-speaking international research centre; and, finally, two had attended another EMI course. One had worked and two had conducted volunteering work and summer camp workshops in English-speaking countries. Twelve had studied French in high school and two had a command of German – no other languages were mentioned in the background questionnaire.

Students were confident enough in English so as to engage in EMI. As one of them stated, 'English doesn't worry me so much because I think I have an apt level'[9] (background questionnaire; 20 November 2017). In fact, some even claimed to be more proficient than the lecturer, as can be seen in statements like:

> We didn't understand some of the questions that the teacher asked us [...] because she didn't pose them clearly due to the English. [...] Today, the teacher's fluency [...] was worse than other days.[10]
> (Audio log; 28 November 2017)

Thus, they seemed to construct the English used in class as 'easy' or 'too easy'. In fact, they sometimes saw it as a hindrance for advanced disciplinary-knowledge attainment, whereby students displayed disengaged identities that envisioned EMI as 'useless', such as:

> If it were in Catalan/Spanish it wouldn't be difficult at all to 'do' the course syllabus that we have covered so far.[11]
> (Audio log; 28 November 2017)

In terms of language expectations, students mentioned 'practising' speaking skills and 'not forgetting' oral comprehension skills, without a clear focus on taking their general English proficiency any 'level' higher, other than learning 'new terminologies in the scientific area that will be important for my professional future'[12] (background questionnaire; 20 November 2017). In this sense, they, like Anna, envisioned English as a strategic 'career skill' which was an asset for academia, and an employability tool for their near future.

Analysis and results: EMI put to action

In the multimodal analysis presented below I contrast the English-only frontstage policy which in theory regulates the class under analysis with the local-language(s) use and plurilingual English practices observed in actual off-, back-, and frontstage interactions. I focus on one instance of informants' compliance to the EMI norms and then on six instances of their whispers of resistance. The former is an interactional frontstage episode where the lecturer introduces the course programme and students ask questions about it in English. The latter include: (1) an episode where the lecturer employs a 'translation-strategy' in Spanish and (2) the students mobilise peer-to-peer clarification requests in Catalan; (3) the lecturer's course calendar involving written plurilingual English forms; (4) a student's personal class notes in plurilingual English forms involving Spanish; (5) an exam with a content question in Spanish; and (6) an episode where the lecturer and six students manage content clarification requests in Spanish during the break. These instances involve the analysis of three pieces of classroom materials, two audio logs, one interview excerpt, and three interactional events dealing with particular EMI teaching/learning classroom strategies taken from ASSEMID's list.

In theory: English only

The lecturer explained the English-only norms of the course under analysis on the first day of class, when she presented the course programme and the assessment tasks. Excerpt 1 below, which reproduces the episode in which she provides the details for an oral presentation assignment, shows that students, like her, also took their compliance to English-only use for granted, unproblematically, as 'self-managed' efficient English-language users 'doing education' in frontstage interactions.

Excerpt 1

@Back:			Classroom. 20 November 2017. Topic: course introduction and task instructions
→	1	*ANN:	the presentation groups I think maybe can be with more students and then less
	2		presentation and just one day instead of two and move the practice maybe # with
→	3		the: -, <or do you think> [?] # move the exam here and then this practice here -, #
		%com:	'here' (twice) is signposted by Anna, on the course plan shown in the screen.
→	4		because is impossible <the> [//] <to> [/] to show you or to teach you animal health
	5		because there are m:any diseases -, many -, the:n what we usually do is you have to
→	6		present <some> [/] some diseases -. I will show you how and then per groups you can
→	7		choose -, I will give you a list and you can choose the disease and prepare like if it
	8		were a congress or a seminar just ten minutes and with the objectives and
	9		introduction and then <the> [//] what you have prepared and then the conclusions +...
→	10	*ST1:	so <animal health is a a class or +...> [?].
→	11	*ANN:	animal health eh <here> [/] here the class is first of all the different types of farms
	12		for an animals and then animal health as animal health diseases.
→	13	*ST1:	uhm.
		%com:	Nodding.

In the teacher-fronted 'procedure-related' (Söderlundh, 2012, p. 96) interaction presented in Excerpt 1, Anna (ANN) displays a 'giving activity instructions' strategy conveying how/when a particular task (an oral presentation) was to be conducted (lines 1–9). She uses repetitions (e.g., 'you can choose' in lines 6–7), paraphrases (line 4; 'to show or to teach') and a non-referential question ('do you think?' seen in line 3) – all conducted in English. Student 1 (ST1) mobilises a 'request for clarification (focus: content)', posing a referential question on the contents for Part 1 (line 10), in an expected sequence of the turn; integrally in English, too. The subsequent 'providing clarification (focus: content)' strategy used by Anna (line 11), where she, too, follows the turn-sequence time of classic question-answer adjacency pairs (Schegloff and Sacks, 1973), is also managed in English, as is the student's last turn with a 'positive-feedback-provision (content)' strategy ('uhm'; line 13). This, along with the English PowerPoint containing the course programme, provided a public, homogeneous 'stage' in English, where the teacher and students mobilised on-task 'doing education' compliant identities as '(self)-Englishised' interactants.

In practice: local language(s) and plurilingual English

Along with compliance, whispers of resistance with breaches of classroom normativities and sociolinguistic comportments emerged which showed that the English-unified 'stage' described above also included subversive language practices and dissenting identities. These emerged not only in back- or offstage talk but also at the frontstage, in what was envisioned as on-task yet 'supplementary' talk, as described below.

The first instance is provided by Anna, who operationalised her non-standard 'local' English in some particular written materials. This is seen in Figure 4.4, which is a PowerPoint that includes the use of 'recuperation' (a plurilingual form of 'resit', as in 'examination retake' from Catalan *recuperació* and/or Spanish *recuperación*). Anna may not have been aware of her use of this particular word, but she claimed that her pedagogical approach to EMI favoured communication over accuracy and to make this point she showed me other instances of her *written* 'Catalan English' (for example, 'at arriving' [from Catalan '*a l'arribar*'], whose standard form is 'upon arrival'). She considered such instances offstage 'let-it-pass' strategies that emerged in quick, written production, the aim being to help the communicative flow of the class. These plurilingual English forms were mostly found in the less formal, quick instructions (e.g., for a farm visit) sent before the class, because the 'official' PowerPoint slides that were shown on-task were spellchecked.

Students displayed similar plurilingual productions in offstage talk, normally for hand-written or computer-mediated notetaking. This is shown in Figure 4.5, which exemplifies how a student made use of non-standard English forms intertwined with Spanish, for the self-provision of short

1 Feb	10-12	Presentations Oestrus Syncronization	B.Serrano
1 Feb	15-19	P6. Visit dairy cow farm	B.Serrano
2 Feb	15-17	SECOND EXAM	B.Serrano
8 Feb	10-12	Recuperation	Nogareda/Serrano

Figure 4.4 Lecturer's whispers of resistance (offstage): Plurilingual English.

Whispers of resistance to EMI policies 85

> Oxytocin from the endometrium (sow), posterior pituitary lobe and corpus luteum (ruminants) promotes prostaglandin synthesis by the uterine endometrium. Dependiendo de la especie, hay otros órganos que producen la oxitocina, aunque en mayor medida se da en la hipófisis.
>
> Prostaglandin diffuses by concentration gradient towards the endometrial capillaries where it drains into the uterine vein, is transported to the ovary and causes luteolysis. Se mueve de la vascularización endometrial a la ovárica.
>
> No conceptus present: Como el embrión no manda señales, disminuye la progesterona. Las prostaglandinas tratan de liberarse siempre. El nivel basal de prostaglandinas es el que hace que se comience la luteolisis, va deteriorando el cuerpo lúteo. Si hay mucha progesterona no hay muchos receptores prostaglandinas ni de oxitocina. Disminuyen los niveles de progesterona por la degradación del cuerpo lúteo, entonces aumentan los receptores de oxitocina, aumenta la prostaglandina y por tanto la degeneración del cuerpo lúteo.

Figure 4.5 Students' whispers of resistance (offstage): Plurilingual English.

summary points and word-for-word translations for what was synchronically being said in class (see, e.g., 'No conceptus present: *como el embrión* [...]').

This offstage performance, which theoretically was a non-staged practice that occurred through the use of personal notebooks and laptops, was systematised by most students. Such on-task 'deviant' productions were for individual purposes. That is, they were treated as transitory draft materials which required off-task 'polishing' or correction before the exam, where the 'terminology' list (which included 'conceptus') had to be properly defined in English. Students reported working on this assessed English glossary off-task, during out-of-classroom time.

Apart from local English forms, Anna also allowed for, operationalised, and, in effect, legitimised, the use of local languages in class, mostly in public teaching/learning spaces that were constructed as belonging to offstage zones. This is illustrated in Figure 4.6, which shows that one of the 'difficult' *content* questions in the exam was provided in Spanish (question number 18) as an 'aid strategy'. I argue that the exam, a personal document to be circulated confidentially (not in the public 'stage') between the students and the lecturer on an individual basis, was a 'fuzzy' offstage area (of strict silence).

17. What is the scrapie? ....and affects the nervous systems of .... (animal species)

18. En los filtros HEPA (High Efficiency Particulate Air) las partículas son atrapadas mediante una combinación de 3 mecanismos? Nombralos

Figure 4.6 Lecturer's whispers of resistance (offstage): Local language use.

The three whispers of resistance presented so far were mobilised for occasional 'pragmatic' or 'utilitarian' purposes. They were justified (i.e. 'authenticated'), for face-saving purposes, as part of a resistant-identity, 'doing student'/'content transmitter' ethos. This ethos prioritised communication at particular times when (momentarily/partially suspended) 'proper' English-only use was deemed a hindrance to effective knowledge transmission/acquisition (see, also, Moore, Borràs and Nussbaum, 2013). Thus, informants still enacted 'doing education' identities by presenting these breaches as exceptions to be made in the English frontstage, with which they engaged by presenting their formal written productions in standard English, as seen, e.g., in exam questions on *language* requiring 'proper' terminology definitions (see question 17 on 'scrapie', in Figure 4.6).

Additional data on the offstage nature of these whispers of resistance was captured in Anna's interview (5 Octoer 2017); when she explained that:

> This year I already told the Head of Studies [...] +" after I will do it [the same class] in Catalan if you don't mind -, for those who did not understand it [...] last year it looks like there were some who didn't get a single thing [...] [this year] nobody stayed [after the first class] and they told me -, +/" no no we understood it].[13]

This provides evidence that monitored 'soft-talk' breaches were framed as occurring outside or aside the classroom 'stage' (here, after class), as an underreported local social contract, only when their 'activation' was required, and with some informal personal notification to departmental authorities but no formal petitions.

I now move to the exploration of resistance acts in actual teacher-student/peer-to-peer classroom interactions. The first example is presented in Excerpt 2, which simultaneously involves a lecturer's frontstage resistance act involving local-language use as well as students' backstage subversive talk, also in local languages.

Excerpt 2

@Back:		Classroom. 28 November 2017. Topic: ovine-caprine
→ 1	*ANN:	after um ah one um a new question 'to lamb' to lamb (3") or lambing <is for ewes>
→ 2		[>] (4") eh <u>parir una oveja</u>.
	%tra:	after um ah one um a new question 'to lamb' to lamb (3") or lambing <is for ewes>

Whispers of resistance to EMI policies 87

→ 3	*ST1 %com: %tra:	[>] (4") eh <u>to have a lamb.</u> <*què diu*> [<] [?] <*què vol dir*> [?] [>] <*pastar*> [?]. whispering. <what is she saying> [<] [?] <what does she mean> [?] [>] <graze> [?].
→ 4	*ST2: %com: %tra:	<*no ho sé*> [<]. whispering. <I don't know> [<].
→ 5	*ST1: %com: %tra: %com:	+^ ah <u>parir una oveja.</u> whispering. +^ ah to have lamb. whispering.

In Excerpt 2, Anna (ANN) begins a teacher-fronted disciplinary-content transmission in English by initiating her turn with a 'display question' (line 1, where she asks for a definition of 'lambing'). In an overlap occurring during a four-second pause, two students get involved in a backstage peer-to-peer 'clarification-request' strategy in Catalan. This was a response to their not understanding the notion being explained. In line 3, Student 1 (ST1) asks Student 2 (ST2) a question and Student 2, also confused, responds in an overlap, whispering 'I don't know' in Catalan (line 4).

After her short pause, and upon obtaining no response by students, Anna uses a 'translation' in Spanish (line 2) as a strategy to avoid a communication breakdown, on perceiving that her point was not understood – her short pause may indicate 'problems arising in the understanding of English' (Söderlundh, 2013, p. 92). Student 1, in a quick latch, acknowledged the effectiveness of the lecturer's clarification (as a feedback-turn response) by repeating Anna's translation (line 5); all-in-all resulting into a successful learning event (for a summary of this interaction see Figure 4.7). I argue that this was a frontstage resistance act because it contravened the established

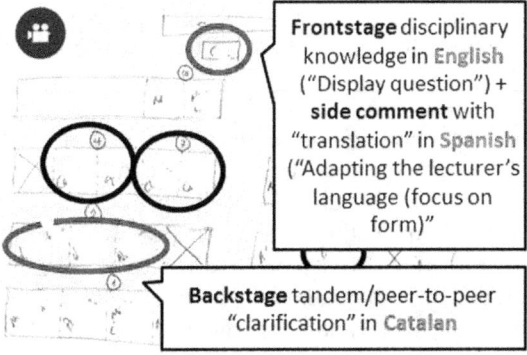

Figure 4.7 Lecturer's frontstage and students' backstage talk involving local languages.

rules that concepts and definitions shall be provided, on-task, in the nominal language of instruction, English, not through 'translation' strategies. Anna showed awareness of this 'slip' with the comment: 'I normally try to say everything in English'.[14]

The interaction in Excerpt 3 below took place during the ten-minute break, in the same classroom. It involved Anna (ANN), who remained in her teacher-fronted position with the screen switched on, and one of the six students, who remained seated (Student 1, ST1). These students used this 'out-of-class' offstage time to initiate content and language clarification questions which they had not asked in the English-only frontstage. I argue that this is so because the break allowed for a non-formal ('suspended-rules') transition time to use local languages, still within the hierarchised classroom setting, when the 'staged' lecture had yet to come to an end.

Excerpt 3

@Back:			Class break. 28 November 2017. Topic: ovine-caprine.
→	1	*ST1:	una cosa # en ad libitum <comen todo lo que quieran o de todo lo que quieran> [?].
		%tra:	one thing # in ad libitum <do they eat as much as they want or everything they want> [?].
	2	*ANN:	+^ no porque tú les das todo hecho.
		%tra:	+^ no because you give them it all prepared.
→	3	*ST1:	vale.
		%tra:	ok.
	4	*ANN:	<eh no> [/] <no viste <en> [/] en la en el video> [?] hacen una preparación es como #
→	5		es como <en en> [//] en las vacas de leche el <el unifeed <es> [/] es venga eso es
	6		extra eh no: es el unifeed +...
			<eh no> [/] <you didn't see in [/] in the in the video> [?] they made a substance it's like # it's like <in in> [//] dairy cows the <the unifeed <is> [/] is ok this is extra eh no: it's the unified +...

Student 1 initiates the turn with a 'question-posing' strategy in Spanish (line 1). By latching, Anna, who also understands the break as 'extra' content/language question-solving time, transmits disciplinary knowledge (on animal feeding) in her 'repetition of explanation (focus: content)', solving the question successfully in Spanish (line 2) (see positive feedback by ST1; line 3). Anna also draws the students' attention to the corresponding video-materials concerning the topic at hand (line 4), through the provision of further details on a particular concept ('ad libitum') in Spanish (lines 4–6). By providing knowledge expansion, she presents herself as a committed

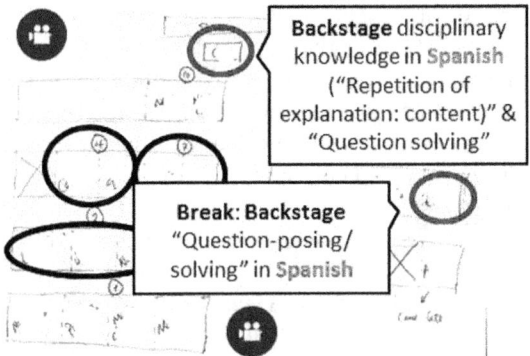

Figure 4.8 Lecturer's and students' offstage talk involving local languages.

specialist '*doing*' 'being a content transmitter'. The 'fuzzy' offstage nature which provided legitimation to local language use with six students needing support during 'interlude' time can be seen when Anna states that the information presented during the break was additional (non-assessed) content information (with 'this is extra'; lines 5–6) (for a summary of this interactional event see Figure 4.8).

On that day, Student 1 in her audio log reported that she had used a local language most of the time and that she, indeed, had had questions on terminology that had been sorted out in Spanish/Catalan. When asked about any remarkable learning/teaching episode involving language, she stated that there had been 'none' ('*ninguno*') – Anna's audio log only mentioned that there had been 'some questions that showed interest', without any comments concerning language choice/use (audio logs; 28 November 2018). This provides further evidence that these resistance acts were normalised in class, as they were common practice and were perceived of, both by the EMI lecturer and students, as part of the (legitimised) routines of 'public-in-private' behaviour, presented as their own extra-time effort to invest in (and to be shown as) 'doing education'.

Conclusion

In this chapter, I have provided a sociolinguistic perspective of EMI in action by problematising the effects of top-down internationalising Englishisation policies upon university agents' bottom-up multilingual classroom management. Departing from a contextualised analysis at a public university in bilingual Catalonia, UdL, I have argued that the critical sociolinguistics angle is fruitful in order to advance into the exploration of theoretical, methodological, and analytical frameworks that help us to unpack the challenges of EMI implementation for non-English 'native' university agents in everyday academic life, in Southern Europe. I have suggested that this approach may offer a more realistic critical-education picture that may inform EMI pedagogies and educational stakeholders about the complex contradictions and tensions that emerge in the operationalisation of EMI in institutions whose routine local norms basically involve local-language(s) use, and where the implementation of English as the *lingua academica* is relatively new.

More specifically, I have departed from the view that 'as a matter of radical strategy, all forms of oppositional behaviour, whether actually resistance or not, must be examined for their possible use as a basis for critical analysis' (Giroux, 1983, p. 291), which I have addressed by proposing, and testing, an exploratory framework that I have called 'whispers of resistance'. I understand this framework as a way to investigate the 'secret' (under-reported) social meanings of the resistance practices and dissenting academic identities whereby those who are led to put EMI into practice display their concerns and problems (e.g., for effective content transmission in EFL) when implementing particular English-language regimes in multilingual EMI classrooms.

Through a micro multimodal data analysis which included video-recorded interactions, observations and reported subject positionings, this has allowed me to provide evidence that educational agents involved in EMI put into question and, in effect, contest the Englishisation mission while, simultaneously, taking up, naturalising, and operationalising it. In this regard, I have shown that lecturers and students are deeply invested in the neoliberal language-in-education tenets which construct languages in outcomes-oriented economic terms, particularly by approaching English as the 'natural' language to rationalise linguistic diversity and as a 'productive' academic skill and necessary professional asset. This explains their displays of compliance acts towards EMI norms, epitomised in the intense language work that they conduct for the self-attribution of efficient communicative proficiency in English – i.e., for neoliberally-minded 'self-Englishisation'. These compliant positionings are grounded on self-managed and self-made English-language user presentations of the rational, self-disciplined self.

By following a Goffman-inspired analytical framework which foregrounds the relevance of educational agents' perceived degree of 'institutionality' (i.e. formality) for particular classroom activities, I have zoomed in on the ways in which these situated practices and identities display engagement with EMI interplay with the resistance acts that lecturers and students unfold in daily practice, on- and off-task. These include conscious

Whispers of resistance to EMI policies 91

and unconscious subversive local-language(s) use as well as non-accidental 'let-it-pass' plurilingual English forms that contravene institutional language directives and classroom normativities, at the back-, off- and frontstage of the hierarchised EMI classroom 'theatre'. I have argued that these whispers are of a 'practical' nature and tend to emerge when the 'content transmission/acquisition' side of EMI is perceived to be put at risk due to ineffective ELF proficiency in language-related events, and/or when the contingencies of particular content-transmission/acquisition, and course procedure-related interactional events require interactants 'to come to the point'. The observed disengaged identities emanating from these resistance acts, consequently, unpack the ways in which educational agents make sense of, and navigate, the contradictions emerging when language-policy regimes clash with actual classroom dynamics. Basically, they present themselves as 'doing education' by taking up 'being a student' or 'content transmitter' academic identities to self-attribute linguistic authority in the successful management of EMI.

While assuming that defining what may count as a form of 'resistance' still remains a difficult task, I conclude that, overall, this paper has provided evidence that resistance in the EMI class is about disrupting 'whispers' that call for, and actually put into action, alternative multilingual language practices based on more balanced, realistic language-in-education pedagogies, in internationalised universities which are guided by the globalised new economy.

Notes

1 All data cited in this chapter is from the project is *Towards an empirical assessment of the impact of English-medium instruction at university: language learning, disciplinary knowledge and academic identities* (ASSEMID), funded by the Spanish Ministry of Economy, Industry and Competitiveness (*El Ministerio de Economía, Industria y Competitividad* – MINECO), code FFI2016-76383-P. 30 December 2016 – 29 December 2019.
2 Spanish is the official language of the Spanish nation-state, and a global language, too. Catalan is the 'original' ('*vernacular*') language of Catalonia which has been socioeconomically and politically persecuted and minoritized, and which has no official recognition in the EU (see Block and Khan, this volume).
3 The data was collected with informed consent and was anonymised, following university ethics and confidentiality protocols.
4 All information in languages other than English was translated by the author. Catalan original: 'Les assignatures que són amb anglès ha de ser totes en anglès -, [...] no pot ser només tenir el PowerPoint amb anglès i <expli> [//] explicar en <catal> [//] i en <cast>,, <vale> [?]. És el que ens han dit la cap d'estudis'.
5 Catalan original: 'Em vaig oferir'.
6 Catalan original: 'Crec jo han de saber una terminologia <clar> [!] perquè després els hi sonaria tot a xino [...] perquè si vols buscar informació d'una cosa

si fas la cerca en català i en castellà és molt # minsa [...] Ara un biotecnòleg [...] tota la recerca que faci ha de ser en anglès [...] amb empreses [...] <de> [//] dedicades a la producció animal -, o la medicina animal'.
7 Catalan original: 'Un anglès català'.
8 Catalan original: 'Tampoc domino tant com per corregir a un alumne'.
9 Spanish original: 'El inglés no me preocupa tanto porque creo que tengo un nivel adecuado'.
10 Catalan original: 'No hem entès algunes preguntes que ens ha fet la professora [...] perquè no les ha formulat de manera entenedora per causa de l'anglès. [...] Avui la fluidesa [...] de la professora ha estat pitjor que altres dies'.
11 Catalan original: 'Si fos en català/castellà ens costaria molt poc fer el temari que hem fet fins ara'.
12 Spanish original: 'Nuevas terminologías en el ámbito científico que serán importantes para mi futuro profesional'.
13 Catalan original: 'Aquest any ja li vaig dir a la de cap d'estudis [...] +" després ho faré [la mateixa classe] en català si no et sap greu -, pels que no s'han entès [...] l'any passat es veu que hi va haver que no es van enterar de res [...] [enguany] no es va quedar ningú i em van dir -, +" no no ja ho hem entès'.
14 Catalan original: 'Normalment procuro dir-ho tot en anglès'.

References

Armengol, L., Cots, J. M., Llurda, E., & Mancho-Barés, G. (2013). *Universitats internacionals i plurilingües? Entre les polítiques i les pràctiques a les universitats de Catalunya*. Universitat de Lleida: Edicions de la Universitat de Lleida, Lleida (Catalonia, Spain).
Benwell, B. M., & Stokoe, E. M. (2002). Constructing discussion tasks in university tutorials: Shifting dynamics and identities. *Discourse Studies*, *4*(4), 429–453.
Benwell, B. M., & Stokoe, E. M. (2005). University students resisting academic identity. In K. Richards & P. Seedhouse (Eds.), *Applying conversation analysis* (pp. 124–139). Houndmills and New York: Palgrave Macmillan.
Block, D. (2018). *Political economy in sociolinguistics: Neoliberalism, inequality and social class*. London: Bloomsbury Publishing.
Bretxa, V., Comajoan, L., & Vila, F. X. (2016). Is science really English monoglot? Language practices at a university research park in Barcelona. *Language Problems & Language Planning*, *40*(1), 47–68.
Codó, E. (2018). Language policy and planning, institutions and neoliberalisation. In J. W. Tollefson & M. Pérez-Milans (Eds.), *The Oxford handbook of language policy and planning* (pp. 467–484). Oxford: Oxford University Press.
Cots, J. M. (2013). Introducing English-medium instruction at the University of Lleida, Spain: Intervention, beliefs and practices. In A. Doiz, D. Lasagabaster & J. Sierra (Eds.), *English medium instruction at universities. Global challenges* (pp. 106–127). Bristol: Multilingual Matters.
Dafouz, E. (2018). English-medium instruction and teacher education programmes in Higher Education: Ideological forces and imagined identities at work. *International Journal of Bilingual Education and Bilingualism*, *21*(5), 540–552.

Duchêne, A., Moyer, M. G., & Roberts, C. (Eds.). (2013). *Language, migration and social inequalities. A critical sociolinguistic perspective on institutions and work*. Bristol: Multilingual Matters.

Firth, A. (1996). The discursive accomplishment of normality: On Lingua Franca English and Conversation Analysis. *Journal of Pragmatics*, *26*(2), 237–259.

Flubacher, M., Duchêne, A., & Coray, R. (2018). *Language investment and employability. The uneven distribution of resources in the public employment service*. Switzerland: Palgrave.

Giroux, H. (1983). Theories of reproduction and resistance in the new sociology of education. *Harvard Educational Review*, *53*(3), 257–293.

Goffman, E. (1959). *The presentation of self in everyday live*. London: Penguin.

Hazel, S., & Mortensen, J. (2013). Kitchen talk – Exploring linguistic practices in liminal institutional interactions in a multilingual university setting. In H. Haberland, D. Lønsmann & B. Preisler (Eds.), *Language alternation, language choice and language encounter in international tertiary education* (pp. 3–30). Dordrecht: Springer.

Lasagabaster, D., Cots, J. M., & Mancho-Barés, G. (2013).Teaching staff's views about the internationalization of Higher Education: The case of two bilingual communities in Spain. *Multilingua*, *32*(6), 751–778.

Llurda, E., Doiz, A., & Sierra, J. M. (2015). Students' representations of multilingualism and internationalization at two bilingual universities in Spain. In A. H. Fabricius & B. Preisler (Eds.), *Transcultural interaction and linguistic diversity in higher education* (pp. 92–115). London: Palgrave Macmillan.

Mancho-Barés, G., & Arnó-Macià, E. (2017). EMI lecturer training programmes and academic literacies: A critical insight from ESP. *ESP Today*, *5*(2), 266–290.

Martín Rojo, L. (2019). The 'self-made' speaker: The neoliberal governance of speakers. In L. M. Rojo & A. del Percio (Eds.), *Language and neoliberal governmentality* (pp. 162–189). London: Routledge.

Moncada-Comas, B., & Block, D. (2019). CLIL-*ised* EMI in practice: Issues arising. *The Language Learning Journal*. doi:10.1080/09571736.2019.1660704.

Moore, E., Borràs, E., & Nussbaum, L. (2013). Plurilingual resources in Lingua Franca talk: An interactionist perspective. In H. Haberland, D. Lønsmann & B. Preisler (Eds.), *Language alternation, language choice and language encounter in international tertiary Education* (pp. 85–102). Dordrecht: Springer.

Mortensen, J. (2014). Language policy from below: Language choice in student project groups in a multilingual university setting. *Journal of Multilingual and Multicultural Development*, *35*(4), 425–442.

Mortensen, J., & Haberland, H. (2012). English-the new Latin of academia? Danish universities as a case. *International Journal of the Sociology of Language*, *216*(216), 175–197.

Piller, I., & Cho, J. (2013). Neoliberalism as language policy. *Language in Society*, *42*(1), 23–44.

Preisler, B. (2014). Lecturing in one's first language or in English as a lingua franca: The communication of authenticity. *Acta Linguistica Hafniensia*, *46*(2), 218–242.

Prieto Martín, A. (2017). *Flipped Learning: Aplicar el modelo de aprendizaje inverso*. Madrid: Narcea Ediciones.

Pujolar, J. (2019). Linguistic entrepreneurship: Neoliberalism, language learning, and class. In L. Martín Rojo & A. Del Percio (Eds.), *Language and neoliberal governmentality* (pp. 113–134). London: Routledge.

Rose, M. R., Diamond, S. S., & Baker, K. M. (2010). Goffman on the Jury: Real jurors' attention to the 'offstage' of trials. *Law and Human Behavior*, *34*(4), 310–323.

Sabaté-Dalmau, M. (2014). *Migrant communication enterprises: Regimentation and resistance*. Bristol: Multilingual Matters.

Sabaté-Dalmau, M. (2016). The Englishisation of higher education in Catalonia: A critical sociolinguistic ethnographic approach to the students' perspectives. *Language, Culture and Curriculum*, *29*(3), 263–285.

Sabaté-Dalmau, M. (2020). Marketing university students as mobile multilingual workers: The emergence of neoliberal lifestylers. *International Journal of Multilingualism*, *17*(1), 11–29.

Schegloff, E., & Sacks, H. (1973). Opening up closings. *Semiotica*, *8*(4), 289–327.

Secretariat for Universities and Research. (2015). University Language Policy. Ministry of Economy and knowledge. Catalan government. Retrieved from http://universitatsirecerca.gencat.cat/en/01_secretaria_duniversitats_i_recerca/universitats_i_recerca_de_catalunya/politiques_i_principals_actuacions/politica_linguistica_universitaria/index.html.

Söderlundh, H. (2012). Global policies and local norms: Sociolinguistic awareness and language choice at an international university. *International Journal of the Sociology of Language*, *216*(216), 87–109.

Söderlundh, H. (2013). Language choice and linguistic variation in classes nominally taught in English. In H. Haberland, D. Lønsmann & B. Preisler (Eds.), *Language alternation, language choice and language encounter in international tertiary education* (pp. 85–102). Dordrecht: Springer.

Spolsky, B. (2019). *The individual in language policy and management*. Càtedra UNESCO de diversitat lingüística i cultural. Barcelona: Institut d'Estudis Catalans. Retrieved from http://www.catedra-unesco.espais.iec.cat.

UCLES. (2001). *Quick placement test*. Oxford: Oxford University Press. University of Cambridge Local Examinations Syndicate.

Appendix 1: Transcription System

Language coding

Plain: English
Italics: Catalan
Underlined: Spanish

Conventions

@Bck:	Background information
%com:	contextual information about the previous turn
%tra:	free translation of turn for languages other than English
#	pause
[/]	repetition
[//]	reformulation
<>	scope
+"	quotation follows
:	lengthened vowel
[…]	Turns omitted for space or confidentiality constraints

Intonation

.	end-of-turn falling contour
?	end-of-turn rising contour
!	end-of-turn exclamation contour
-,	intra-turn fall–rise contour

5 NOT English teachers, except when they are

The curious case of oral presentation evaluation rubrics in an EMI-in-HE context[1]

David Block and Guzman Mancho-Barés

Introduction

English-medium instruction (EMI) lecturers in a range of higher education (HE) contexts tend to remain faithful to the identities they developed in their respective academic disciplines, the sites in which 'the important interactions in a professional's life occur, bringing academics, texts, and practices together into a common rhetorical locale', and where 'members...see themselves as having some things in common and being, to some extent, similar to each other' (Hyland, 2012, p. 25). In this sense, EMI lecturers position themselves as deliverers of disciplinary content, whose job is to teach a body of knowledge to their students and socialise them into the relevant 'discourse formations' (Foucault, 1989) and disciplinary communities to which they themselves belong. In addition, as we see in research carried out in a range of contexts worldwide (e.g. Aguilar, 2017; Airey, 2012; Costa, 2013; Karakaş and Bayyurt, 2019; Wilkinson, 2013), they tend, when asked, to avoid dealing with duties associated with English language teaching, such as focusing explicitly on syntax, morphology, pronunciation, and technical vocabulary; attending to language functions or disciplinary genre; and the provision of language feedback and correction. These behaviours are seen as outside the realm of what is expected of them and what they are willing to do. Nevertheless, EMI lecturers sometimes contradict this version of events, by citing language as a part of their taught content (e.g. Baker and Hüttner, 2019; Basturkmen, 2018) and more importantly, by clearly focusing on the above listed language-related components (Block and Moncada-Comas, 2019; Dafouz, Hüttner and Smit, 2016; Moncada-Comas and Block, 2019).

In this paper we show how this attention to language occurs in what might be considered an extremely minute part of what constitutes EMI in

STEM – the use of rubrics to evaluate oral presentations given by students. As we shall see, while such rubrics contain items addressing content, that is, knowledge of the subject matter of the course being followed, they also contain items that might reasonably be classified as related to language learning and also teaching. Our interest here is in these items: (1) in and of themselves, as evidence that these EMI lecturers do take into account their students' English language proficiency when evaluating their oral presentations; and (2) as potential mediators of classroom exchanges that focus on aspects of the English language. Our research questions are thus:

- Are there elements in the oral presentation evaluation rubrics used by lecturers that may be described as language-related? If so, what elements?
- How are oral presentation evaluation rubrics operationalised in the classroom, that is, how do they mediate the feedback provided by lecturers to students?

We begin with a short discussion of evaluation rubrics in education in general, and in EMI in particular, our intention being to make clear the object of our focus here. We then provide information about our research and the two lecturers whose use of oral presentation rubrics are examined in this chapter. This done, we proceed to analyse, in order: (1) the rubrics; (2) how the lecturers explain their origin and purpose; and (3) how the rubrics mediate the feedback provided by the two lecturers when their students give oral presentations. We close with answers to our research questions within a discussion of issues arising from our research.

Background

Stevens and Levy (2005, p. 3) have defined rubrics used for the assessment of student work as follows:

> At its most basic, a rubric is a scoring tool that lays out the specific expectations for an assignment. Rubrics divide an assignment into its component parts and provide a detailed description of what constitutes acceptable or unacceptable levels of performance for each of those parts.

According to Reddy and Andrade (2010), in its simplest form a rubric takes the shape of a grid, and contains four elements: (1) a list of the component parts to be assessed, also known as 'dimensions' (i.e. skills or knowledge) in its leftmost column; (2) a column for every performance level to be assessed; (3) a scoring strategy for levels of performance (normally a numerical scale) in the top row; and (4) descriptions of the levels of performance appearing in the grid. Other types of rubric are known as 'scoring guide' rubrics, which contain only a description of the highest level of performance. Further classifications of rubrics distinguish between holistic and analytical rubrics: in the former, instructors make overall judgements about the students' quality of performance, while in the latter, instructors rate the student performance according to several assessment dimensions (Jonsson and Svingby, 2007). Other types of rubrics include task/topic-specific versus generic, with the former deemed to be a more reliable assessment method than the latter as it produces more generalisable and dependable scores, despite being more time-consuming to prepare (Wiggins, 1998).

If we examine publications surveying the use of rubrics in formal education, such as Reddy and Andrade (2010), which focus on the use of rubrics in HE, and Panadero and Jonsson (2013), which focus on the use of rubrics for formative purposes across all educational levels, we see that most studies to date are student-based, concentrating on students' attitudes and responses. This means that there is a relative shortage of studies examining the teacher's side of rubric use, which is our interest here. In addition, most publications on this topic have mainly focused on HE in general and there has been very little work on the specific context of EMI. Where there has been an interest in EMI, and, in addition, the teacher side of rubric use, researchers such as Dimova and Kling (2018) and Gundermann and Dubow (2018) have examined the use of rubrics to assess EMI lecturers' English language proficiency. Although this is no doubt an important issue in EMI research, it is not directly relevant to our focus here, as we aim to explore issues arising in the ways that rubrics are used by EMI lecturers. For example, Ball and Lindsay (2013) explore the issue of 'assessment fairness', arguing that non-native speaker students taking an EMI course may be seen to be in a linguistically unfavorable position compared to their native-speaker classmates.[2] Ball and Lindsay suggest that one way to remedy this problem is to use rubrics as a means of formative assessment, which means an emphasis is placed on student progress. This approach stands in marked contrast to a one-off assessment at the end of a course, which does not allow any consideration of whether or not – and how – a student has improved. Meanwhile, in another publication relevant to our research here, Breeze and Dafouz (2017) focus on the pedagogical implications of rubrics in EMI, as they may be used as a tool for students to develop specialised communication skills and disciplinary content simultaneously. The authors suggest that 'language teachers could provide support with language to both sets of agents, by helping teachers design rubrics that take the language component into account and students in performing and integrating the different and complex CDFs [Cognitive Discourse Functions] appropriately' (Breeze and Dafouz, 2017, p. 89).

Finally, there is an issue relevant to the use of rubrics as assessment tools that transcend education contexts, namely, their potential 'washback effect', whereby the evaluation criteria are a (or *the*) starting point for the curriculum. Thus, they directly shape taught content, materials used, teaching methodologies employed, and the classroom activities that emerge thereof (Alderson and Wall, 1993). As Andrade (2005, p. 27) has observed:

> Whether we teach elementary school or graduate students, rubrics orient us toward our goals as teachers. We use them to clarify our learning goals, design instruction that addresses those goals, communicate the goals to students, guide our feedback on students' progress toward the goals, and judge final products in terms of the degree to which the goals were met.

The question that arises in the case of oral presentations in EMI classrooms is whether or not and how rubrics are exploited according to Andrade's list of uses. Thus, if students are to be evaluated for the analysis of data that they present, or the more technical matter of how they use PowerPoint, or, what concerns us most here, how competent they show themselves to be as users of English, then it would make sense for lecturers to create opportunities for students to practise these aspects of oral presentations and provide formative feedback, if possible. Later in this chapter, we will return to this link between what is done in class sessions during a course and what is assessed at the end, when students give oral presentations. We will also be concerned with other issues arising in this short review of rubrics, such as the purpose of rubrics (according to the lecturers using them) and their specific content, especially in relation to the balance between items focusing on disciplinary knowledge and items devoted to aspects of communication and language use.

The research

In this chapter we focus on data from three sources. The first of these consists of excerpts taken from transcriptions of classes taught by the two lecturers at the centre of our discussion. In principle, classes were taught integrally in English, although both Catalan and Spanish were used on occasion, especially by students. The second source of data is the oral presentation rubrics used by the lecturers to evaluate the oral presentations that their students gave at the end of their courses. These have been slightly adapted for presentation in this chapter and one of them, written in Catalan, has been translated into English by the authors. The third and final source of data in this chapter is an interview that the authors, Guzman Mancho-Barés and David Block, carried out with three lecturers participating in the ASSEMID project (see Chapter 1 of this volume) – Raquel, Miquel, and Jaime.[3] This interview, which lasted approximately 100 minutes, took place and was audio recorded on 19 February 2019. It focused on the three lecturers' use of oral presentation evaluation rubrics. In this chapter, for reasons of space, we concentrate only on comments made by Raquel and Miquel. Both the lecturers and the two interviewers spoke in Catalan during the interview, and in this paper we provide English translations of all excerpts reproduced. These interview excerpts, and the classroom data presented in this chapter follow transcription conventions that are listed and glossed in the Appendix.

In our analysis of the data, our main concern is key words related to the research questions outlined previously. We thus focus on the occurrence of words and phrases associated with language teaching and learning, such as 'pronunciation', 'fluency', 'correct language', and 'vocabulary', and how they are used in the three data sets examined – the rubrics, the interview about rubrics and classroom interaction mediated by the rubrics. We are also interested at a broader level in how, across these three data sets, Raquel and Miquel position themselves as particular types of professionals, namely, as STEM lecturers teaching in English who show a strong affiliation to their disciplinary identities (Hyland, 2012), even if they also inadvertently (and perhaps despite themselves) show an interest in English language learning.

Drawing on the work of Harré and his colleagues over the years, we understand positioning as 'the discursive process whereby people are located in conversations as observably and subjectively coherent participants in jointly produced storylines' (Davies and Harré, 1999, p. 37). Here, 'discursive processes' may be understood as interactions involving one or more interlocutors, 'conversations' may be understood as structured sequences of multimodal communicative acts, and 'storylines' may be understood as the ongoing narrative that emerges and evolves as conversations unfold. One aspect of positioning theory that is particularly relevant in this study is the notion of rights and duties (and we would add responsibilities). As Harré (2004, p. 4) explains, 'rights and duties are taken up and laid down, ascribed and appropriated, refused and defended in the fine grain of the encounters of daily lives'. In this chapter, we see how our two participants, Raquel and Miquel, draw clear boundaries around, and defend their rights and duties as discipline-based professionals, avoiding the prospect that they might, on some occasions, and in some capacity, act as language specialists. In the next section, we provide more information about Raquel and Miquel.

EMI lecturers and their teaching

At the time of the study, Raquel and Miquel were both in their mid-forties and had been working as full-time lecturers at the University of Lleida for eight and nine years, respectively. They both had three years' experience as EMI lecturers and both claimed to have, at a minimum, C1 English competence (as established by the Common European Framework Reference for Languages, Council of Europe, 2020). They regularly engaged in a range of English-mediated activities, such as giving papers at international conferences and participating in exchange activities in which English was the chief medium of communication. Their attitude towards EMI in general, and specifically their activity as EMI lecturers, was positive. Indeed, neither was critical of the idea of teaching content in English or their participation in this activity. Raquel and Miquel explained that they had become EMI lecturers of their own volition – out of professional curiosity and perhaps a desire to accept and meet a challenge. They reported that they were not enticed by incentives, such as a reduction in academic workload, and that they did not feel that they were pressured to take on this responsibility. In effect, they saw EMI as a necessary part of the university's internationalisation programme (see the introduction to this volume), which they subscribed to fully, and in the classes that we observed, they both seemed very much at ease when teaching in English.

The first lecturer, Raquel, is an agronomy engineer whom we observed while she taught an undergraduate course on animal biotechnology in Autumn 2017. There were 20 students on this course, all of whom were Catalan/Spanish bilinguals. The research team conducted four interviews involving Raquel and observed her teaching on nine occasions. The observations revealed that her teaching methodology was primarily lecturer-led, with accompanying PowerPoint and frequent pauses for questions initiated by both lecturers and students. The following classroom excerpt is a part of longer exchange that occurred in one of Raquel's classes. It provides a glimpse of how she handled question-and-answer exchanges.

Classroom excerpt 1

1. RAQ: how do you store samples?/if you want to extract DNA and you/collect the samples today from a net-necropsy/whatever/how do you store-store those samples?/
2. S1: minus twenty degrees/
3. RAQ: **a** minus twenty degrees in a freeze in a normal freezer/ yeah/**a** minus twenty is a good temperature/now how do we-we da-da/how will we order them?/which one goes first?/which would be the first thing that you will do?/

4. S2: [collect/
   5. S3: [collect/
   6. RAQ: collect samples/very good/so I've got the samples and then what do I- what do I do with those samples?/
   7. S2: store/
   8. RAQ: you store them/what's next?/
   9. S3: lyse/
   10. RAQ: we lyse the cells because we need to free/that DNA/with a buffer/now that we have all the cells broken eh in-in an/you have like a soup of all the components/what do you need to do?/first of all=
   11. S4: =remove/ehrm RNA/
   12. RAQ: first you remove the RNA/with an RNase/and now that you got rid of the RNA what's next?/you need to remove the rest of the things that are not good/ that are not DNA in the cell/

(Raquel, 21 September 2017)

We have four observations to make about this exchange, which was fairly typical of what occurred in Raquel's classes. First, it shows how Raquel's students were engaged with Raquel's teaching and that they felt comfortable and confident enough to intervene and provide answers to her questions. Second, it shows Raquel's effectiveness as a lecturer in English as she deftly uses an IRF (Initiation-Response-Feedback) pattern as a way of eliciting responses. A third observation is that Raquel maintains English as the mediator of all classroom activity and ensures that her students hear the key terminology that they need in English. Indeed, on all occasions when Raquel was observed, she seldom deviated from the English-only norm and when students addressed her in Catalan or Spanish, she almost always responded in English. Fourth and finally, and despite the fact that Raquel resisted any attempt by researchers to position her as an English-language teacher (Block, 2020; Block and Moncada-Comas, 2019; Mancho-Barés and Aguilar-Pérez, 2020), we observed that when her students produce word-length utterances in the response phase of IRF exchanges, she then models lengthened versions of these responses in the feedback phase: 'collect' (4/5) → collect samples' (6); 'store' (7) → 'you store them' (8); and 'lyse' (9) → 'we lyse the cells' (10). And when S4 does utter something resembling a phrase, 'remove ehrm RNA' (11), latching this to Raquel's 'first of all' (10), Raquel still provides a lengthened alternative: 'first we remove' (12).

In addition to exchanges such as the one reproduced above, Raquel sometimes organised group activities in preparation for the oral presentation. However, beyond a statement at the beginning of the course that all classroom activity was to be done in English, Raquel seldom took effective measures to ensure that her students spoke English on these occasions. In this situation, local students tended to use their L1(s) when communicating during group work, while they would use English when addressing Raquel. As we see in the excerpt above, these interactions might involve little more than a phrase or two, which means that by far the most extended interventions by students took place on the day that they gave their oral presentations in five groups of 3–4 students.

These oral presentations were the final stage of a project in which students had to submit a written assignment and a leaflet focusing on different topics relevant to the creation of animal biotechnological-based protocols: animal parentage, the origin of milk, babesiosis (a malaria-like parasitic disease), a global meat company, and the diagnosis of psittacosis (a pneumonia or typhoid fever-like illness) in caged birds. However, between the phrase-length IRF exchanges with Raquel and the group work in which English was very rarely used, there was little classroom time devoted to the production of more extended stretches of text in English. This means that Raquel's students went into their presentations less prepared than they would have been if there had been more opportunities to communicate in English about the topics covered in the course.

The second lecturer focused on in this chapter is Miquel, an infrastructure engineer who was observed while he co-taught a highly technical undergraduate course on facilities and infrastructures in spring 2018. There were 13 students enrolled on this course, all of whom were Catalan/Spanish bilinguals. As with Raquel, Miquel was involved in four interviews and he was observed teaching on eight occasions. These observations revealed one extremely noteworthy feature of Miquel's classes, namely, that the virtual entirety of class time was devoted to lecturer-led explanations of engineering problems that had previously been assigned as homework. Making extensive use of the whiteboard, Miquel would generally take students through different formulas step-by-step on the way to solutions, with explanations lasting up to 20 minutes. Periodic attempts on his part to include students, either by asking individual students directly or by soliciting questions via the hopeful invitation 'any questions?', generally led to short answers and silence, respectively. Thus, instead of IRF exchanges, there were initiations leading to minimal responses, which led to confirmation that a response was correct (or incorrect).

As regards English as the medium of instruction, Miquel maintained this language in both his explanations of problems and the few occasions when students posed questions. His students, meanwhile, were seldom if ever observed using English amongst themselves, although it is worth noting that there were no group activities requiring them to speak to each other in any of the eight classes observed. The upshot of this state of affairs is that a student could attend Miquel's classes without ever speaking a word of English. The exception to this pattern was the last day of the course, which was devoted to oral presentations given by groups of 2–4 students. These presentations were based on group projects in which students developed a model solar thermal plant. Students were expected to prepare for these presentations on their own, which they did in self-organised meetings. However, given the lack of opportunities to use English in class, Miquel's students went into this final activity even less prepared than Raquel's students.

As we have observed in this section, Raquel and Miquel's classes unfolded with very different interactive dynamics, with Raquel providing more space for her students to intervene. Nevertheless, in both cases we are in the realm of a teacher-centred approach to the transmission of knowledge and the few opportunities that students had to speak in English (more in Raquel's classes than in Miquel's classes) cannot be considered sufficient in-class preparation for oral presentations requiring the delivery of long stretches of discourse in English. Yet, students were expected to be able to do just this, and their performance was assessed using oral presentation evaluation rubrics. It is to these rubrics that we now turn.

The rubrics

As noted above, we see rubrics as instructional artefacts embodying particular attitudes and beliefs about what is important and what is not important in the assessment of students. In what follows, we unpack the content of the rubrics by identifying and analysing key words related to language and communication. This process allows us to see to what extent language and communication are goals in these lecturers' teaching. We begin here with the rubric employed by Raquel to assess her students' oral presentations. This rubric consists of eight dimensions against which presenters are assessed on a 1–5 scale, where there is a progression from a poor performance (1) to an excellent performance (5). The form, which was written in English, is reproduced in Table 5.1 below.

One key question in our minds was the origin of the rubrics, that is, how lecturers came to use the rubrics they used to assess their students' presenting skills. Raquel reported that she had colleagues who used rubrics for assessment, and this led her to consider using one herself. In the end, she created her own rubric, basing it on one sent to her by a colleague and an online search for ideas about rubric preparation. It should be noted that the information she found was about disciplinary content and not language issues. Her main criterion as she prepared her rubric was 'ease of use', given that in her classes, she asked her students to assess other groups' presentations

Table 5.1 Raquel's rubric

Criteria	Below expected level (1–2)	At expected level (3–4)	Above expected level (5)
1. Clarity: introduction of topic	Topic introduced.	Topic introduced clearly, and purpose of talk was made clear.	Topic introduced clearly, and interesting way. Purpose of talk was made clear. Outline of points was given.
2. Clarity: organisation of the talk	The message is so disorganised you cannot understand most of the message. The organisation of the message is mixed up and random.	The message is organised. The listener has no difficulty understanding the sequence and relationships among the ideas in the message.	The message is overtly organised. The speaker helps the listener understand the sequence and relationships of ideas by using organisational aids such as announcing the topic, previewing the organisation, using transitions, and summarising.
3. Clarity: visual aid	Poor, distracts audience, and is hard to read. Adds nothing to presentation.	Thoughts articulated clearly, but not engaging.	Visual aid enhances presentation, all thoughts articulated and keeps interest.
4. Length of time	Far too long or too short.	More or less within expected time.	Perfect timing!
5. Non-verbal skills: eye contact	Does not attempt to look at audience at all, reads notes the entire time.	Student maintains eye contact most of the time but frequently returns to notes.	Student maintains eye contact with audience, seldom returning to notes.
6. Non-verbal skills: Enthusiasm	Shows absolutely no interest in topic presented.	Occasionally shows positive feelings about topic.	Demonstrates a strong positive feeling about topic during entire presentation.

(*Continued*)

Table 5.1 Continued

Criteria	Below expected level (1–2)	At expected level (3–4)	Above expected level (5)
7. Delivery: voice – clarity, pace, fluency	The pronunciation is unclear. The speaker exhibits many 'ahs', 'uhms' or 'hemmm'. The listener has difficulty understanding the message.	The volume is not too low or too loud and the rate is not too fast or too slow. The pronunciation is clear. The speaker exhibits few 'ahs', 'uhms', or 'hemmm'.	The speaker delivers the message in a confident, poised, enthusiastic fashion. The volume and rate varies to add emphasis and interest. Pronunciation is clear.
8. Knowledge: response to questions	Not all questions could be answered. Questions answered with difficulty, and little knowledge of the topic was demonstrated.	Most questions answered. Answers showed good knowledge and understanding of the topic. Language was mainly correct.	Questions answered with little difficulty. Very good knowledge of the topic was demonstrated. Language was correct and fluent.

using the same rubric. Here, we will not focus on these student peer evaluations, as our exclusive interest is in Raquel and how she used her rubric.

In Raquel's rubric, all items arguably relate to language and communication, with the first four items focusing on the organisation of content and time, the following three items focusing on verbal and non-verbal communication, and the final item focusing on the display of topic knowledge. The items most clearly related to language teaching and learning are (1) 'Clarity: introduction of topic'; (2) 'Clarity: organisation of the talk'; and (7) 'Delivery: voice – clarity, pace, fluency'. The first two are important because they are about key characteristics of text, such as cohesion (the key notion of 'organisation') and coherence (the equally important notions of 'clarity' of purpose and of audience 'understanding'). Meanwhile, item seven is especially significant because it focuses on pronunciation and fluency, two key aspects of language learning and teaching. When interviewed about the items in the rubric, Raquel systematically described what each one was about before concluding as follows:

Interview excerpt 1

so there is a more content-based part/a part more about/knowing how to convey information/having a non-visual contact etcetera/and afterwards I like to tell them that they have to know how to speak in public/ even if this stresses them out a lot/

As for item seven, where language teaching and learning criteria come to the fore more explicitly, she commented:

Interview excerpt 2

the first/the delivery / ... then there's fluency that you have/also clarity so you're not emmm emmm emmm the whole time/

At another point in the interview, Raquel was asked to explain exactly what she meant by 'Delivery: voice – clarity, pace, fluency'. The following exchange ensued.

Interview excerpt 3

1. DAV: what exactly does this mean?/fluency and-and all of this/ you've put this here/examples/haven't you?/of what it is not/
2. RAQ: yes/interrupting the speech with a lot of pauses/but above all pronunciation is that/I come across participants who memorise a paragraph to say something/and they say it without pronouncing **anything**/and I am saying that I can't understand anything they say/there is no way the others can understand anything because-because I am not able to say where one word has started and where the other has ended/
3. DAV: right
4. GUZ: can you think of any examples?/do examples come to mind?
5. RAQ: okay *abcdefg directly* {NB *abcdefg* = a series of random, meaningless syllables}
6. DAV: okay okay
7. RAQ: so they go and say *abcdefg the answer*/and you say *I don't know exactly what the hell she said*/
8. GUZ: so it's about vocalising right?/
9. RAQ: yes/
10. GUZ: not so much to say *table* instead of *teibəl*/
11. RAQ: no no/that would be/.../it's one thing after another/

108 *David Block and Guzman Mancho*

Here, Raquel refers to how some students memorise and then recite their presentations, a point she had raised earlier in the interview, when she explained that this could be a strategy for students who do not have a sufficient command of the information they are presenting. She also suggests that when students do this, they are incomprehensible as they run their words together or, what is worse, they produce utterances which one hears as a string of random, meaningless syllables with real words interspersed. When asked for an example (turn 4), she produces two (turns 5 and 7, respectively), first imitating a student rushing through a series of such syllables followed by the word 'directly' and then imitating another student doing the same before uttering 'the answer'. This leads to the introduction of the term 'vocalising' to describe what Raquel is talking about (turn 8), which is not about the correct pronunciation of individual words (turn 10), but the calm and clear enunciation of, as Raquel puts it, 'one thing after another' (turn 11).

As noted previously, Raquel consistently denied ever acting as an English language teacher in her classes; rather, she framed any focus on language identified by researchers as being about the teaching of disciplinary knowledge that the students needed to have as veterinary specialists. Her clear positioning as *NOT an English-language teacher* comes through in the following comment, when she responds to a question about how she uses her rubric to assess students' performances:

Interview excerpt 4

so the only thing I penalize them for is if they are not able to communicate/because in this case they have not managed to pass on to me the knowledge/this concept/that I have asked them to explain/where it comes up on an exam for example/and I have to penalize them/but I couldn't care less if they say it in a broken or Shakespearean way/

Raquel's claim that she does not care if students speak 'broken English' as long as their communication could be seen as somewhat consistent with her behaviour in the classroom, as we see above in classroom excerpt 1. There, Raquel seemed to want her students to produce phrase-length responses to her questions instead of one, two or three-word utterances.[4]

Moving to the oral presentation evaluation rubric used in Miquel's course, we see that it consists of nine key points, all of which are assessed according to an ascending 0–10 scale. Below, in Table 5.2, we have translated these nine items into English from the original in Catalan.

When asked about the origin of his rubric, Miquel explained that it was after his first interview with the ASSEMID research team that he began to think about the possibility of evaluating oral presentations by means

Table 5.2 Miquel's rubric

Criteria for rating an oral presentation

(1) (0–10) Structure of the presentation: the structure is correct and follows a logical order of the work carried out (introduction, objectives, methodology and results, conclusions, etc.)
(2) (0–10) Quality of the oral expression: during the presentation, the student demonstrates the ability to explain, speak calmly, and with eloquence.
(3) (0–10) English quality: the student constructs sentences correctly, which are rich in vocabulary and easily understood, with good pronunciation.
(4) (0–10) Quality of transparencies: they are clear, understandable, and show the use of a variety of resources.
(5) (0–10) Variety of resources employed: different resources (models, videos, images…) that help improve audience understanding of the concepts explained.
(6) (0–10) Adaptation of the presentation to the stipulated time: the presentation has not exceeded the specified time.
(7) (0–10) Correct results: the results are correct and show that students have worked and understood them.
(8) (0–10) Quality of the answers to the questions posed by the examiners: the answers are appropriate, respond coherently to the questions, and show a profound knowledge of the subject.
(9) (0–10) Synthesis of the presentation: the presentation synthesises the work developed in a suitable way.

of a rubric. At this time, Miquel remembered how several years earlier, while teaching at another HE institution, he had used a rubric to evaluate his students' final year projects, which included oral presentations delivered in English. He recovered this rubric, adding to it the ninth category – 'Synthesis of the presentation'. Miquel reported that he found the 1–10 scale useful and easy to manage, although when he saw Raquel's rubric during the interview, he said that he found her glosses of the different evaluation bands useful and that this was something that he would think about doing with his own rubric in the future.

A close reading of Miquel's rubric shows how several of the items are about the presentation itself – '(4) Quality of transparencies'[5] and '(6) Adaptation of the presentation to the regulation time'. Meanwhile, others are about content or content communication – '(5) Variety of resources employed'; '(7) Correct results'; '(8) Quality of the answers to the questions posed by the examiners'; and '(9) Synthesis of the presentation'. Finally, and what is also releveant to this study are the other items which may be situated in the realm of language teaching and learning –'(1) Structure of the presentation'; '(2) Quality of the oral expression'; and '(3) English quality'. In these latter three items, we see an interest in, respectively, the structure of discourse (and indeed disciplinary genre), speaking fluently and a command of key formal aspects of English (sentence grammar, vocabulary and pronunciation). In addition, Miquel has introduced the sub-criterion 'vocabulary richness' to assess his students' accurate use of terminology. However, when it was suggested to Miquel that items 1–3 were, in effect, language teaching and learning criteria, he responded as follows:

Interview excerpt 5

anyway it's true that/that it's a somewhat subjective criterion/because we/what we were saying/we aren't linguistic experts/but it's something that you notice right off/ that student who speaks clearly/who vocalises/ who tries to express ideas/who connects sentences/I mean you see it/ on the other hand the other one who says something from memory/who without any effort for/even what he/she is saying/pronounces it correctly/because it's very easy now to go to google/repeat this right?/in addition these are technical words from the project/that you say these/ you have to say them right/I don't know/a conjunction/or a verb that/ but the key words/you have to pronounce them correctly/because it's what you have been working on here/and sometimes in my case/a lot of students come with crib notes/I mean I saw that/they just read right?/or they try to do without but they don't remember/so they go there and/or course it's a very poor impression right?/

In this response, Miquel opens with a disclaimer, stating clearly that he and his fellow EMI lecturers are not 'linguistic experts', and that they use 'subjective' criteria when evaluating their students' oral performances. Part of this subjective criteria is no doubt captured in his claim that the difference between a good presentation and a bad presentation is 'something that you notice right off'. Nevertheless, throughout this response he refers to language use when he refers to speaking clearly, trying to express ideas, connecting sentences, and using conjunctions and verbs correctly. It is noteworthy that he uses the term 'vocalising' and inserts the notion that it is not good for students to memorise their presentations and then recite them, something which Raquel also mentioned (see interview excerpt 4 above). In this sense, Miquel aligns himself with Raquel as a fellow EMI lecturer who imparts disciplinary knowledge but not English-language knowledge. Importantly, Miquel explicitly positions himself as an infrastructure engineer whose responsibility and duty is to teach discipline-specific language. He thus relates all of the language-specific issues mentioned to disciplinary discourse, using arguments such as 'these are technical words from the project' or 'it's what you have been working on', as the goal is to create a good 'impression' as a trainee infrastructure engineer.

Thus far, we have presented background information about Raquel and Miquel, briefly discussed their teaching, and then focused on the rubrics that they used to evaluate their students' oral presentations. Regarding these rubrics we see how, despite continued claims to the contrary, both lecturers have included in their assessment criteria elements that clearly are language-oriented and therefore are arguably in the realm of English language teaching. Nevertheless, a rubric is a pedagogical artefact, an inert graphic representation of a particular approach to teaching and learning and above all, the result of decisions (implicit or otherwise) that have been taken about what is important or not important in an oral presentation. What is needed is an examination of how the rubric comes to life (or is brought to life) when students give their oral presentations and lecturers make their comments on what they have observed. In the next section, we discuss how Raquel and Miquel responded to their students' oral presentations and how these responses relate to rubric content.

Operationalising rubrics

As explained above, Raquel's students gave their presentations in groups of three or four. An examination of Raquel's comments on her students' performances on that day reveal something of a surprise in that she did not make one single comment relating to items 5–7 on the evaluation rubric: neither the non-verbal skills of eye contact (item 5) and enthusiasm (item 6), nor the delivery items – voice clarity, pace and fluency (item 7). Instead, she limited herself to operationalising items 1–3, that is, the 'clarity' items having to do with the introduction and coverage of the topic, the organisation of the presentation and the use of visual aids, and item 8, that is, displaying knowledge through the answering of questions. Actually, she addressed this latter item by encouraging students to ask questions and by asking questions herself. The following two comments are fairly typical of those made by Raquel on this occasion.

Classroom excerpt 2

when you have a …/that have quite a high level of inbreeding/so that they keep the puppies to be mothers and the puppies to be fathers/and there's a lot of inbreeding a lot of of/might be that some of the puppies are close/so close together that maybe they get a very very similar or even identical marker sets/so that the profile/the DNA profile that they get/is identical between two brothers/what could you do then?/

(Raquel, 15 January 2018)

Classroom excerpt 3

in your leaflet you have a/small chart on the biggest (…) of flood/of food fraud okay?/and about a quarter/about 25% of the fraud are in olive oil/about 25 of frauds more or less are in milk/and twelve per cent are on honey/how can you make fraud of honey?/I have no idea/I'm just asking/.

(Raquel, 15 January 2018)

In marked contrast to Raquel, Miquel did make comments about his students' language and therefore addressed items 2 and 3 in his rubric on 'Quality of the oral expression' and 'English quality', respectively. In the following excerpt, Miquel invokes the notion of 'correct English', focusing specifically on lexical selection, to point out an error in a group's PowerPoint slide:

Classroom excerpt 4

watch out when you write in English/write in correct English/there is for instance here/playback/instead of payback okay?/so make sure you are writing/the right words/you can always use the/the correctors/your correctors etcetera/.

(Miquel, 24 May 2018)

On another occasion, he focused on one student's lack of enthusiasm, which he related to the student being incomprehensible or lacking coherence during his presentation:

Classroom excerpt 5

sometimes you were a little bit/I don't know/when you were talking your enthusiasm was too plain/sometimes it was difficult to understand your ehrm/your reasoning/ because you were too like/you need/you lacked a little bit of enthusiasm okay?/some more energy on that/

(Miquel, 24 May 2018)

Still feeding back to the same group of students, Miquel went on to a new topic, interrupting others when they are speaking:

Classroom excerpt 6

some of you have not to interrupt your your classmates or your colleague in this cases/It's not nice that he is saying something/and you said something to complement/if he's if he's not sure you can help/but he's talking don't interrupt him/because it gives an impression that of unreliability or something like that/

(Miquel, 24 May 2018)

In the following excerpt, Miquel calls out a different group of students for a series of errors committed during their presentation:

Classroom excerpt 7

things that should improve in your presentation/formally okay?/in formal aspects/that have things to improve/for instance/you were reading most of the time okay?/probably because you were not/eh/sure enough with your English in general/ that doesn't give a good impression on your/on your xxx/you were also not staring at the audience/so we didn't see each other/we were just/I don't know looking at the wall/and at the same time as you were projecting your voice to that place/and instead of to us/it was difficult to listen to you/you were/you had especially you NAME/you had to speak up a little bit/your voice were too low / it was difficult to understand what you were saying/you were not projecting to our place and your voice were a bit low/so it was difficult to understand what you were saying/

(Miquel, 24 May 2018)

Here, Miquel expresses strong criticism of these students' performance. He first criticises them for reading their presentation, although he allows that they perhaps did so because they 'were not sure enough with [their] English'. Reading is deemed to be bad for two key reasons: first, it leads to a lack of eye contact with the audience – 'not staring (sic) at the audience' and 'looking at the wall' – and second, it leads to poor voice projection and low volume, making it 'difficult to understand what [students] were saying'. In this instance, Miquel seems to be operationalising criterion two from his evaluation rubric – 'Quality of the oral expression' – to rate the group's performance. Importantly, these comments are the kind of comments that an English-language teacher might make when assessing a student's oral performance, even if, we imagine, most English-language teachers today would probably not use such direct language. Indeed, it is hard to see the feedback provided by Miquel as formative in any way for these students given how harsh it was and the fact that it was not accompanied by any suggestion of alternative strategies that students might have adopted. Further to this, it is somewhat surprising that Miquel focuses so explicitly on the interplay between non-verbal skills (eye contact), oral delivery, and intelligibility, when in his classes students had been given practically no opportunity to hone the skills that he criticises them for lacking. In contrast, Raquel might well have weighed in on language issues, as she certainly had at least acknowledged that they are important as part of disciplinary knowledge when pushed to discuss the topic in the interview. However, as we observed above, on this occasion she said nothing about language or even communication more broadly.

Discussion and final remarks

The previous sections show evidence of the extent to which the assessment of language is foregrounded by Raquel and Miquel, despite asserting that assessing student language proficiency is not their duty as EMI lecturers. Specifically, the first research question is about the presence (or lack thereof) of language-related elements in the evaluation rubrics. As explained above, the language content assessed is related to phonology ('the pronunciation is clear'), morpho-syntax and lexical items. A stance towards language correctness is glimpsed in the descriptors, as in the case of Miquel's descriptor number three: 'English quality: the student constructs sentences correctly' (see Table 5.2 above). This performance-based descriptor used by Miquel is resonant of debates about assessment fairness in non-native EMI settings where measures are taken to balance the language-concept demands on lower-proficient students' English (Ball and Lindsay, 2013). Other items in the two rubrics deal with language use in general and the mastery of fluency (basically the avoidance of hesitations or false starts), as well as discourse organisation. Thus, in Raquel's rubric there are key words and phrases such as 'speaker exhibits many "ahs", "uhms"… ' or 'the organisation of the message is mixed up and random' for lower student performance levels, which show, at least to some extent, that student language proficiency is being assessed. The general description of language forms and language use is completed with extra-linguistic factors related to non-verbal communication and prosody, making Raquel's rubric a very comprehensive one, indeed, to the extent that it might also be used in a more mainstream, general English-language teaching setting.

In relation to the second research question – about the provision of feedback mediated by rubrics – class observation transcripts shed light on two different practices. On the one hand, content feedback is the only type of feedback given by Raquel, despite the fact that her rubric *did* list language-related dimensions and three levels of performance, as mentioned above. It is outside the scope of this chapter to explore the reasons why Raquel did not provide feedback on language issues to her students on the day in question; what matters, we believe, is the educational consequence of such practice. That is to say, by *not* providing language-related feedback to students, Raquel may have activated a negative washback effect, whereby students left the session unaware of their shortcomings as users of specialised discourse in English. From a formative assessment point of view, the provision of this type of feedback would have been helpful for students when preparing future oral presentations in English. On the other hand, Miquel did provide language-related feedback directly related to items in his rubric. This practice is very welcomed from an English-language teaching and learning point of view in that it constitutes a formative assessment that is language (and communication) focused. It is also potentially a case of positive washback effect in terms of language learning, even if, as we suggested above, we are not sure how useful Miquel's (arguably harsh and direct) feedback would be to his students. Still, by providing feedback on what he saw as his students' linguistic deficiencies, Miquel at least takes a step in the direction of promoting student language and communication awareness, and, in contrast to Raquel's students, his students may have left the session with a better idea of how to improve their performance the next time they are asked to prepare and give an oral presentation in English.

Nevertheless, there is no evidence to suggest that the rubrics used by Raquel and Miquel exercised any kind of washback effect on their teaching. As we observed above, neither of them provided students with sufficient practice for oral presentations; in particular, there was a lack of opportunities to produce extended stretches of discourse in English. Indeed, on the whole Raquel and Miquel do not seem to have thought very much, if at all, about how their teaching practices might be linked to assessment procedures in ways that are both consistent and effective. In this regard, we are reminded of an observation made some two decades ago by a group of researchers about the lack of professional training available to science faculty members at universities in the US:

> Science faculty members have little, if any, professional training in teaching at the college level. An instructor with years of classroom seat time and graduate assistant teaching experience may have the equivalent teaching expertise of a football fan...with some experience in pick-up football ... He or she would not likely be hired to play in a

professional football league. Effective teaching involves the purposeful, research-informed development of innovative lessons actively involving students in learning.

(Sunal et al., 2001, p. 247)

Our observations of Raquel and Miquel's uses of rubrics to assess their students' oral presentations leads us to a similar conclusion. There is thus the need for a greater provision of teacher development programmes focusing on pedagogical and assessment procedures in EMI contexts (cf. Breeze and Dafouz, 2017), as well as the creation of peer support groups, in which EMI lecturers could meet and discuss their EMI experiences. There is also the potential here to adopt a broader view of what is at stake and what occurs when rubrics are used in EMI to evaluate students' oral presentations. For example, drawing on research on 'academic literacies' (e.g. Lea and Street, 2006), we might see the rubrics used by Raquel and Miquel as depositories of itemised technical skills (how to give an oral presentation) and language knowledge (how to give an oral presentation in English), but also as more subtle embodiments of discipline-bound positions for students to occupy (how to act like a veterinarian or an infrastructure engineer). This is because, when Raquel and Miquel provide more impressionistic than well-thought-out rationalisations for the content and use of their rubrics, they are invoking a kind of 'feel for the game' that they already have and that their students need to develop. This means there is all the more reason for these and other EMI lecturers to think about what goes into these rubrics and above all, how they are part of a broader process whereby students are socialised into their respective academic disciplines.

Notes

1 All data cited in this chapter is from the project is *Towards an empirical assessment of the impact of English-medium instruction at university: language learning, disciplinary knowledge and academic identities* (ASSEMID), funded by the Spanish Ministry of Economy, Industry and Competitiveness (*El Ministerio de Economía, Industria y Competitividad* – MINECO), code FFI2016-76383-P. 30 December 2016 – 29 December 2019.
2 Of course, this claim refers exclusively to the use of English, given that these students are, at a minimum, bilingual and therefore not linguistically disadvantaged in the least.
3 These are pseudonyms.
4 Although it is also quite possible, as Sarah Khan (personal communication) has suggested, that she was merely confirming her students' responses in her own words.

5 The use of 'transparencies' here perhaps means that the rubric that Miquel adopted was first conceived when presenters used overhead projectors. The understanding here seems to be that 'transparencies' is a proxy for PowerPoint slides, as all students did their presentations using PowerPoint.

References

Aguilar, M. (2017). Engineering lecturers' views on CLIL and EMI. *International Journal of Bilingual Education and Bilingualism*, *20*(6), 722–735.

Airey, J. (2012). "I don't teach language": The linguistic attitudes of physics lecturers in Sweden. *AILA Review*, *25*, 64–79.

Alderson, C., & Wall, D. (1993). Does washback exist? *Applied Linguistics*, *14*(2), 115–129.

Andrade, H. G. (2005). Teaching with rubrics. The good, the bad and the ugly. *College Teaching*, *53*(1), 27–30.

Baker, W., & Hüttner, J. (2019). 'We are not the language police': Comparing multilingual EMI programmes in Europe and Asia. *International Journal of Applied Linguistics*, *29*(1), 78–94.

Ball, P., & Lindsay, D. (2013). Language demands and support for English-Medium instruction in tertiary education. Learning from a specific context. In A. Doiz, D. Lasagabaster & J. M. Sierra (Eds.), *English-medium universities* (pp. 44–61). Bristol: Multilingual Matters.

Basturkmen, H. (2018). Dealing with language issues during subject teaching in EMI: The perspectives of two accounting lecturers. *TESOL Quarterly*, *52*(4), 692–700.

Block, D. (2020). Using a version of positioning theory to show how identity is made in interaction. In W. Ayres-Bennett & L. Fisher (Eds.), *Multilingualism and identity: Interdisciplinary perspectives* (pp. TBD). Cambridge: Cambridge University Press.

Block, D., & Moncada-Comas, B. (2019). English-medium instruction in higher education and the ELT Gaze: STEM lecturers' self-positioning as NOT English language teachers. *International Journal of Bilingual Education and Bilingualism*. doi:10.1080/13670050.2019.1689917.

Breeze, R., & Dafouz, E. (2017). Constructing complex cognitive discourse functions in higher education: An exploratory study of exam answers in Spanish- and English-medium instruction settings. *System*, *70*, 81–91.

Costa, F. (2013). 'Dealing with the language aspect? Personally, no.' Content lecturers' views of teaching through English in an ICLHE context. In S. Breidbach & B. Viebrock (Eds.), *CLIL in Europe: Research Perspectives on policy and practice* (pp. 117–127). Bern: Peter Lang Publishing.

Council of Europe. (2020). Global scale – Table 1 (CEFR 3.3): Common reference levels. Retrieved July 31, 2020, from https://www.coe.int/en/web/common-european-framework-reference-languages/table-1-cefr-3.3-common-reference-levels-global-scale.

Dafouz, E., Hüttner, J., & Smit, U. (2016). University teachers' beliefs of language and content integration in English-medium education in multilingual settings. In T. Nikula, E. Dafouz, P. Moore & U. Smit (Eds.), *Conceptualising integration in CLIL and multilingual education* (pp. 123–143). Bristol: Multilingual Matters.

Davies, B., & Harré, R. (1999). Positioning and personhood. In R. Harré & L. van Langenhove (Eds.), *Positioning theory* (pp. 32–52). London: Sage.

Dimova, S., & Kling, J. (2018). Assessing English-medium instruction lecturer language proficiency across disciplines. *TESOL Quarterly, 52*(3), 634–656.

Foucault, M. (1989 [1972]). *The archaeology of knowledge*. London: Routledge.

Gundermann, S., & Dubow, G. (2018). Ensuring Quality in EMI: developing an assessment procedure at the University of Freiburg. *Bulletin VALS-ASLA, 107*, 113–125.

Harré, R. (2004). Positioning theory. Retrieved from www.massey.ac.nz/~alock/virtual/positioning.doc.

Hyland, K. (2012). *Disciplinary identities*. Cambridge: Cambridge University Press.

Jonsson, A., & Svingby, G. (2007). The use of scoring rubrics. Reliability, validity and educational consequences. *Educational Research Review, 2*(2), 130–144.

Karakaş, A., & Bayyurt, Y. (2019). The scope of linguistic diversity in the language policies, practices, and linguistic landscape of a Turkish EMI University. In J. Jenkins & A. Mauranen (Eds.), *Linguistic diversity on the EMI campus: Insider accounts of the use of English and other languages in universities within Asia, Australasia, and Europe* (pp. 96–122). London: Routledge.

Lea, M.R., & Street, B.V. (2006). The "Academic Literacies" model: Theory and applications. *Theory into Practice, 45*(4), 368–377.

Mancho-Barés, G., & Aguilar-Perez, M. (2020). EMI lecturers' practices in correcting English: Resources for language teaching? *Journal of Immersion and Content-Based Education.* doi.org/10.1075/jicb.19011.man.

Moncada-Comas, B., & Block, D. (2019). CLILised EMI in practice: Issues arising. *Language Learning Journal.* doi:10.1080/09571736.2019.1660704.

Panadero, E., & Jonnson, A. (2013). The use of scoring rubrics for formative assessment purposes revisited; A review. *Educational Research Review, 9*, 129–144.

Reddy, Y. M., & Andrade, H. (2010). A review of rubric use in higher education. *Assessment and Evaluation in Higher Education, 35*(4), 435–448.

Stevens, D., & Levi, A. J. (2005). *Introduction to rubrics: An assessment tool to save grading time, convey effective feedback, and promote student learning.* Sterling, VA: Stylus Pub.

Sunal, D. W., Hodges, J., Sunal, C. S., Whitaker, K. W., Freeman, L. M., Edwards, L., Johnston, R. A., & Odell, M. (2001). Teaching science in higher education: Faculty Professional Development and Barriers to Change. *School Science and Mathematics, 101*(5), 246–257.

Wiggins, G. (1998). *Educative assessment.* San Francisco, CA: Jossey-Bass Publishers.

Wilkinson, R. (2013). English-medium instruction at a Dutch University: Challenges and pitfalls. In A. Doiz, D. Lasagabaster & J. M. Sierra (Eds.) *English-medium instruction at universities: Global challenges* (pp. 3–24). Bristol: Multilingual Matters.

Appendix

Table 1 Transcription conventions

Convention	Function
/	Forward slash indicates natural pauses between units of speech.
I thi-I think	Hyphen used to indicate hesitation.
italics	Double voicing oneself or another person; imitating another person.
underlined	In the class excerpts, anything not said in English is underlined.
bold	Words uttered with emphasis.
[xxxx [xxxx	Overlapping speech.
=	Latching – an utterance by one speaker flows seamlessly into the following utterance by another speaker.
{ xxx }	Extra-linguistic activity is described in curly brackets.
?	Rising intonation (as in a question).
xxx	Phonetic transcription of a word.
(…)	Incomprehensible.

6 The secret life of English-medium instruction unraveled

Sarah Khan

Introduction

By examining EMI at two Catalan universities and bringing into view its less conspicuous features, Chapters 2–5 of this book shed further light on EMI practices at a time when EMI is becoming firmly established in HE worldwide. At this point, grassroots research initiatives, such as the one documented in this book, can make an impact both locally and globally in moulding the shape of EMI to come. The chapters in this book have played their part in advancing EMI research, bringing to light the workings of little-known and, at times, abstruse microphenomena which have been essential in detecting contradictions between top-down institutional policies and actual EMI implementation. In Chapter 2, Elisabet Arnó and Marta Aguilar examine why students choose either an EMI or an L1 course when given the choice and why the lecturer chooses to teach in English. Arnó and Aguilar voice concerns about unsystematic course planning which, among other outcomes, leads to in-service lecturers volunteering for EMI and a lack of preparation or framework for students. They also point to the absence of collaboration between ESP and EMI teachers and course difficulty levels being a strong deterrent for students signing up for EMI courses. In Chapters 3, 4, and 5, which move into the EMI classroom, we see how the authors have complemented the findings of multiple data sources with real-time classroom observations. In Chapter 3 Balbina Moncada-Comas has described the multimodal resources students use as they interact in the EMI classroom and how students navigate the lesson by alternating between distinct identities. Moncada-Comas points out the many rich forms of communication at play in the classroom, which go beyond the spoken language. In Chapter 4 Maria Sabaté-Dalmau has employed a critical sociolinguistics framework for understanding the dynamics in the EMI classroom, highlighting the plurilingual nature of the EMI classroom and how lecturers and students use local languages as well as non-standard forms of

The secret life unraveled 121

English. Sabaté-Dalmau also exemplifies how EMI stakeholders adhere to neoliberal tenets and questions the validity of such thinking and its repercussions in HE and society. Finally, in Chapter 5, Guzman Mancho-Barés and David Block unpack oral presentation rubrics, demonstrating how EMI lecturers include language parameters when evaluating students' spoken production, despite their claims that they do not see themselves in the role of an English-language teacher. The authors also identify inconsistencies between the rubrics the lecturers employ and the feedback and preparation they provide for their students. In effect, while students receive little, if any, guidance on how to conduct presentations, they are nevertheless required to produce ones which align with the items in the evaluation rubrics.

The rationale for this volume was to disseminate the ASSEMID research project[1] findings, and although data was collected in a very specific STEM context at two Catalan universities, many interrelated themes have emerged which could resonate in settings worldwide and provide a basis for new research directions. Therefore, the aim of this concluding chapter is to address seven of the themes identified by the different contributors as key to EMI: (1) equality of learning opportunities; (2) lecturer self-selection; (3) plurilingualism; (4) multimodal communication; (5) disciplinary complexity; (6) low use of English by students; and (7) the role of language in education. I reconsider EMI through these frames of reference, discussing the answers we have found, and the multiple challenges arising.

Equality of learning opportunities

The perpetuation of social inequality has emerged as a recurring theme in the European-based EMI literature (Macaro, 2018; Phillipson and Skutnabb-Kangas, 2013; Shohamy 2013; Wilkinson 2013) but has also been highlighted further afield (Hu and Lei, 2014; Piller and Cho, 2013) and was the principal finding of an EMI case study at a Chinese University (Hu and Lei, 2014). The unfairness of EMI has been identified at other levels of education, for example in the literature on CLIL and bilingual schools (Bruton, 2013; Cummins, 2013) and on a global level it has been highlighted as particularly damaging in countries where extremes of inequality already exist (Block, 2018; Phillipson and Skutnabb-Kangas, 2013).

An example of empirical research which illustrates this has been conducted by Lueg and Lueg (2015). Drawing on the work of Bourdieu (1997), and by using a questionnaire and structural equation modelling, they demonstrated that undergraduate students who choose EMI over DMI (Danish-medium instruction) for a degree in Economics and Business Administration tend to be from higher social classes and have higher perceived English proficiency. Considering the generally high level of English proficiency in Denmark, it's surprising that only 13–23% students chose EMI in this study. This low proportion is comparable with 16% of Spanish students choosing EMI in Arnó and Aguilar's study (Chapter 2), indicating that such an occurrence is not limited to a particular local context. Lueg and Lueg's (2015) study provides evidence that a student's social background affects their choice of language of instruction and, more surprisingly, that students from lower social classes believe EMI to be a greater obstacle, despite having equally high English proficiency as those from higher social classes. These findings have extremely important implications, as they suggest that incentives for improving English language proficiency will not necessarily lead to more students choosing EMI and that further incentives – ones which consider students' class background and foster positive self-efficacy beliefs – also need to be taken into consideration at policy level for all students to benefit.

Arnó and Aguilar (Chapter 2) and Sabaté-Dalmau (Chapter 4) echo other voices from EMI, sociolinguistics, bilingual education, and CLIL research that claim EMI is elitist and is benefitting only a small sector of students. We see this as Arnó and Aguilar find comparatively low numbers of students are signing up for EMI and Sabaté-Dalmau finds that both the EMI teacher and the students in her study embody neoliberal identities. Coming from more privileged backgrounds, these students start EMI a step ahead with better levels of English (acquired from extra tuition, foreign travel, and study experiences) and possibly even higher levels of literacy in the academic discipline being taught thanks to their greater linguistic and cultural capital (Bourdieu, 1997). In other words, they gain advantage through greater previous exposure to and familiarity with formal academic discourse inherited, for example, from parents, who are doctors, lawyers, or engineers. Just as some universities are providing special support measures for disadvantaged groups of students (e.g. from low income backgrounds or with physical disabilities) so should they recognise the heighted polarization EMI causes and provide pre-EMI language support, counselling on both a social and academic level, and appropriate in-class scaffolding (multilingual resources, focus on form, interaction, diversifying assessment) to mitigate these inequalities (Van der Walt and Kidd, 2013). The issue of equality extends to EMI lecturers as well, as I shall argue in the following section.

Lecturer self-selection

There are, by now, a good number of reports on lecturers' perceptions of different aspects of EMI (e.g. Aguilar and Rodriguez, 2012; Başıbek et al., 2014; Tatzl, 2011; Werther et al., 2014), such as its value for teaching and learning, lecturers and students' English proficiency, or lecturers' training needs.

However, little has been mentioned about EMI lecturer selection criteria. One exception is Werther, et al. (2014), who in their article on Danish lecturer perceptions, discuss staff selection for EMI, staff certification schemes for existing lecturers, or including language requirements when hiring staff. Nevertheless, they do not examine lecturer 'self-selection'. Very little research seems to have been carried out on this particular question, which unexpectedly, opens up a Pandora's box of unanswered questions.

One key question worth investigating is whether lecturer self-selection or volunteering for EMI is a recognised practice and part of institutional policy or is 'off the record'. The existence of this practice has been made explicit in all four chapters of this volume. In Arnó and Aguilar in Chapter 2, Moncada-Comas in Chapter 3, Sabaté-Dalmau in Chapter 4, and Block and Mancho-Barés in Chapter 5, lecturers were not specifically hired to teach EMI but were existing lecturers who volunteered to teach a subject they already taught in Catalan or Spanish in English. EMI courses seem to be provided bottom up, depending on whether lecturers agree to teaching in English, rather than top-down programme planning informed by educational goals.

A second question for further research could reveal if self-selected lecturers in other contexts have equally extensive teaching and research experience abroad, as the ones documented in these studies. Clear commonalities were found amongst the lecturers' profiles in these studies. The lecturers had differing years of experience but in all four studies they were multilingual in at least three languages (Spanish, Catalan, and English), with at least a C1 (CEFR) level in English, had had regular international experiences, and were firm supporters of EMI and internationalization processes (see also Dearden and Macaro, 2016; Unterberger, 2014).

If self-selection is as standard a practice as we suspect, and the volunteering lecturers fit in with the profiles described here, the next question would be to find out what it means for the lecturers who do not volunteer for EMI. In the same way that EMI acts as a gatekeeper, keeping out a certain sector of students (Shohamy, 2013) as described in the previous section, does self-selection cultivate elitism and harmful competition amongst academics? Would it unfairly set back the professional development of lecturers teaching in local languages? Answers to these questions would certainly help to create fairer institutional policies and ensure fairer practice in staff training and development. Training (Sánchez-Pérez, 2020) takes on a particularly important supportive role, especially if few or no EMI directives are provided and the onus of EMI implementation is placed on lecturers who, left to volunteer for EMI, carry it out as they deem fit. So far, it seems like existing social inequalities determine the kinds of lecturers and students that enlist in EMI. How these principle agents play out their roles in the classroom is addressed in the following sections.

Plurilingualism

Research on the influence of neoliberal economics on EMI (Codó, 2018; Hadley, 2015; Piller and Cho, 2013) certainly provides serious food for thought on the negative social consequences of implementing EMI, such as severe competition, or elitism as discussed in previous sections. In Chapter 4 Sabaté-Dalmau works from a critical sociolinguistics perspective and makes use of Goffman's *frontstage* and *backstage* metaphor, showing through interview data that both the students and the lecturer identify with neoliberal education tenets (Bourdieu, 1997), seeing English as an essential tool for employability and success in a future career in science or scientific research. Students had extensive prior learning experience of English in private schools or while studying or working abroad, and lecturers had international teaching or research experience, showing that both parties adhered to this neoliberal vision, advocating internationalisation and Englishisation processes. Similar profiles were found for the EMI stakeholders in the other chapters of this volume, which are reflected in the views of Carles, an EMI coordinator at the UdL cited in Chapter 1 (Block and Khan, this volume).

Nevertheless, the *frontstage* and *backstage* metaphor leads Sabaté-Dalmau to propose a framework of 'whispers of resistance' which allows her to take a snapshot of the elements of EMI course implementation where actors stray from their adherence to these neoliberal identities and the English-only norm, either consciously or unconsciously, using local languages (L1 Spanish or Catalan) or non-standard forms of English. The plurilingual nature of the classroom comes to the fore, in a positive sense, as the teacher and students employ their plurilingual resources on task (in presentation slides, students' notes, peer-to-peer interaction, and even in the course exam) to avoid communicative breakdown via the least linguistic resistance (Söderlundh, 2012). These plurilingual 'whispers' were noted in the other three studies in this volume, although in all cases classes were predominantly in English. Thus, we see the English-only norm is maintained in the frontstage of the classroom where the lecturer dominates, but broken in the backstage, where the L1 languages (Catalan, Spanish) are in use.

A recent paper based on interviews and surveys with plurilingual and Dutch EMI lecturers in the Netherlands by Duarte and Van der Ploeg (2019) provides a succinct overview of research on plurilingualism in HE, showing that it is an area which is gaining momentum (e.g. García, 2009). Their findings suggest that plurilingual lecturers were able to engage more with their students through a better appreciation of their shared plurilingual resources, which were believed to improve conceptual understanding, develop a sense of inclusiveness, foster participation, and clarify meaning as well as overcoming the challenge of teaching and learning through

English and compensating for lecturers' lack of knowledge of alternative teaching methodologies. These seem, therefore, convincing arguments to foster plurilingualism in the EMI classroom and readjust the notion that EMI is 'English only'. In practice, EMI involves communication in English among other languages, and, as we will see in the following section, other forms of communication.

Multimodal communication

The studies described in these chapters have shown not only the plurilingual nature of EMI but that an array of other modes of communication are also at play. A multimodal approach (Block and Moncada-Comas, 2019), as taken by Moncada-Comas in Chapter 3, is ultimately essential for a more fine-grained understanding of communication in the EMI classroom. Moncada-Comas rewinds to the beginning of a fleeting episode in the EMI classroom, narrates the episode in depth using Goffman's *frontstage* and *backstage* framework and, moving us through in slow motion, unravels a whole microcosm at work run by socially-defined norms. Moncada-Comas brings our attention to the multimodal nature of students' peer-to-peer interaction (gestures, eye contact, gaze, facial expressions) which illustrates how students self-position in the backstage 'being a student' role (students refraining from interacting with the teacher, showing a lack of enthusiasm and joking) and the frontstage 'doing education' role (students engaging in academic discourse, answering the lecturer's questions, and helping each other work out discipline-related issues). In other words, an awareness of social identity can help us understand these multiple non-verbal forms of on-task communication as it gives us a more rounded understanding of how students construct meaning. Further research would shed light on how these social dynamics could be harnessed to benefit the learning environment in EMI.

Disciplinary complexity

So far, we have seen that students and teachers employ their plurilingual and multimodal resources to enhance communication in the classroom but when do they employ these strategies? In Chapter 2, Arnó and Aguilar, in line with others (e.g. Jenkins, Cogo and Dewey, 2011), suggest that they are related to adherence to cultural identity or when faced with the challenge of disciplinary complexity (Ackerley, 2017; Jiang, Zhang, and May, 2019), as reported in this study by Hu and Lei (2014, p. 560) carried out at a Chinese University:

> One of the two EMI professors (EMI/T2) we interviewed shared with us that he had to code-switch to Chinese when explaining difficult

concepts or teaching challenging content because to use English exclusively would inhibit him from conveying disciplinary knowledge effectively. In particular, he noted that 'in order to help students better understand some complex concepts, I often use illustrative examples from their daily life, and it is more effective to use Chinese in such cases'.

Arnó and Aguilar mention that the complexity of the discipline being taught confounds teaching and learning. In their study both lecturer and students refer to the difficulty of learning advanced electronics, let alone learning it in English. Students call for EMI classes in less complex subject matters and identify the lecturer's effective teaching skills as being essential for them to grasp the subject's complexity. As discussed in this chapter, plurilingual and multimodal teaching methodologies may also be the kind of tools that would mediate this disciplinary complexity.

Low use of English by students

Canadian French immersion studies have shown that students tend to gain receptive skills (reading and listening) and may reach native-like proficiency in them, but this is not so for productive skills (speaking and writing). As Hellekjaer (2006) argues, such settings are analogous linguistically to EMI in universities where the minor language (English) is being used to learn academic content and has restricted use and input, while surrounded by the major languages of everyday use, in this case, Catalan and Spanish. Drawing parallels, in the studies in this volume there seems to have been a paucity of student interventions in English. In Moncada-Comas' study (Chapter 3) the lecturer uses mainly English as the medium of instruction, with a sprinkling of L1 Catalan. Students, in contrast, rarely speak English, using L1 (Catalan or Spanish) among themselves, and when interacting with the lecturer they speak in English providing short responses. After an EMI class, Sabaté-Dalmau (Chapter 4) points out that 'On that day, student 1 in her audiolog reported that she had used a local language most of the time'. Block and Mancho-Barés report similar findings with students using L1 in group work and uttering short phrases in English when addressing the lecturer. Indeed, in the case of one lecturer they observed, Miquel, they state that 'a student could attend ... classes without ever speaking a word of English'.

From the perspective of second language acquisition, students are receiving plenty of input in English in these classes, which involve mainly lecturing. They grapple with difficulties in understanding through L1 peer-to-peer interaction so that it becomes comprehensible (Krashen, 1985) to them, but they are not producing the pushed output (Swain and Lapkin, 1995) necessary to develop their L2 competences in production skills. It could be argued, taking Block and Mancho-Barés's study as an example, that students can be given a chance to use English by giving oral presentations. However, the authors point out that although students were assessed on their oral presentations, they had in fact not been given any time to practise them or to engage in extended discourse in class. These findings suggest that time needs to be set aside in the EMI classroom, so that students can practise becoming proficient both orally and in writing in the discipline at hand.

Effective EMI, therefore, seems to involve maintaining a delicate balance between exposing students to the disciplinary discourse in English (lecturing), using plurilingual and multimodal resources, if necessary, to get across difficult concepts, but most importantly for learning English, giving students a chance to use the language of the discipline themselves.

The role of language in education

EMI lecturers do not actually consider themselves language teachers (Airey, 2012; Baker and Hüttner, 2019; Moncada-Comas and Block, 2019). The EMI construct is superimposed onto them by language specialists, but lecturers see themselves solely as specialists in their respective disciplinary fields, for example, as engineers or biologists, remaining faithful to their disciplinary identities (Hyland, 2012). Is it too much to expect EMI lecturers to recognise that they have a role in addressing English language issues as well? We believe that the answer to this question is 'no'. The question brings us to the concept of language in education (Silver and Lwin, 2013) and how language shapes teaching and learning irrespective of the discipline being taught. From this perspective, *all* teachers are language teachers because language and disciplinary content are inseparable and cannot be contemplated independently (Airey, 2012).

EMI researchers have observed this phenomenon in action, particularly in relation to subject-specific vocabulary, which lecturers consider disciplinary rather than language-related (Baker and Hüttner, 2019; Basturkmen, 2018; Block and Moncada-Comas, 2019; Dafouz, Hüttner, and Smit, 2016; Moncada-Comas and Block, 2019). However, in Chapter 5, Block and Mancho-Barés observe lecturers going beyond the teaching of subject-specific vocabulary by applying language-related criteria (e.g pronunciation, discourse organization or fluency) in assessing their students' presentations.

Both lecturers provide language-related criteria on rubrics as part of their assessment of students' presentations and one lecturer gives immediate language-related oral feedback. In effect, there is mounting evidence in the EMI literature that in teaching through their disciplines, EMI lecturers draw attention to language issues.

Final reflections

The findings described in these chapters have come from specific EMI in STEM contexts in Catalonia, but in this chapter I have attempted to show that the themes that have emerged are relevant to HE around the world. In Chapter 4 of this volume the sociocritical perspective of EMI provided by Sabaté-Dalmau brings our attention to the broad sweep of EMI as she relates it to internationalisation and the top-down influence of neoliberal language-in-education policies on EMI programme coordinators, lecturers, and students. These influences explain the motivations of lecturers and students participating in EMI and determines their profiles (international experience, good command of languages, belief that EMI will bring better prospects), (Chapters 2–5), as well as why students refrain from EMI, because of course difficulty or low English proficiency (Chapter 2). Apart from adhering to neoliberal tenets, lecturers strongly identify with their own disciplines (Chapter 5), and dismiss their role as language educators – unaware of how they use language to initiate students into the discourse of their disciplines. English dominates the frontstage of EMI classrooms (Chapters 3, 4, 5) but unofficial L1 languages have a resolute presence, not only in off-task socialisation but in on-task transmission and construction of disciplinary knowledge as both lecturers and students use the L1 to prioritise effective communication over the use of 'English only'. In fact, we have also seen that communication doesn't stop with languages, but is accompanied by various multimodal resources (Chapters 3 and 4).

Most significantly, and what becomes apparent from the chapters in this volume, is that a detailed focus on microphenomena does not rule out being able to grasp the bigger picture in EMI. In fact, this multi-dimensional approach to research reflects the broad and complex nature of EMI coherent with the sociolinguistic theory of English-medium education in multilingual university settings (EMEMUS) as described by Dafouz and Smit (2016; 2020) and illustrated in their ROAD-MAPPING framework (see Chapter 1). Although there is still a long way to go in unravelling all the secrets of EMI, this kind of approach may prove to be a powerful tool appealing, not just to applied linguistics research, but across disciplines and institutional levels, acting as a catalyst for effective change, collaboration and management of EMI.

Note

1 *Towards an empirical assessment of the impact of English-medium instruction at university: language learning, disciplinary knowledge and academic identities*, funded by the Spanish Ministry of Economy, Industry and Competitiveness (*El Ministerio de Economía, Industria y Competitividad* – MINECO), code FFI2016-76383-P. 30 December 2016–December 2019.

References

Ackerley, K. (2017). What the students can teach us about EMI and language issues. In K. Ackerley, M. Guarda & F. Helm (Eds.), *Sharing perspectives on English-medium instruction* (pp. 257–284). Bern: Peter Lang Publishing.

Aguilar, M., & Rodríguez, R. (2012). Implementing CLIL at a Spanish university: Lecturer and student perceptions. *The International Journal of Bilingual Education and Bilingualism*, *15*(2), 183–197.

Airey, J. (2012). 'I don't teach language'. The linguistic attitudes of physics lecturers in Sweden. *AILA Review*, *25*(25), 64–79.

Baker, W., & Hüttner, J. (2019). 'We are not the language police': Comparing multilingual EMI programs in Europe and Asia. *International Journal of Applied Linguistics*, *29*(1), 78–94.

Başıbek, N., Dolmacı, M., Cengiz, B. C., Bür, B., Dilek, Y., & Kara, B. (2014). Lecturers' perceptions of English medium instruction at engineering departments of higher education: A study on partial English medium instruction at some state universities in Turkey. *Procedia-Social and Behavioral Sciences*, *116*, 1819–1825.

Basturkmen, H. (2018). Dealing with language issues during subject teaching in EMI: The perspectives of two accounting lecturers. *TESOL Quarterly*, *52*(4), 692–700.

Block, D. (2018). *Political economy in sociolinguistics: Neoliberalism, inequality and social class*. London: Bloomsbury Publishing.

Block, D., & Moncada-Comas, B. (2019). English-medium instruction in higher education and the ELT Gaze: STEM lecturers' self-positioning as NOT English language teachers. *International Journal of Bilingual Education and Bilingualism*. doi:10.1080/13670050.2019.1689917.

Bourdieu, P. (1997). The forms of capital. In A. H. Halsey, H. Lauder, P. Brown & A. S. Wells (Eds.), *Education, culture, economy, society* (pp. 46–58). Oxford: Oxford University Press Books.

Bruton, A. (2013). CLIL: Some of the reasons why… and why not. *System*, *41*(3), 587–597.

Codó, E. (2018). Language policy and planning, institutions and neoliberalisation. In J. W. Tollefson & M. Pérez-Milans (Eds.), *The Oxford handbook of language policy and planning* (pp. 467–484). Oxford: Oxford University Press.

Cummins, J. (2013). Bilingual education and Content and Language Integrated Learning (CLIL): Research and its classroom implications. *Revista Padres y Maestros/Journal of Parents and Teachers*, *349*, 6–10.

Dafouz, E., Hüttner, J., & Smit, U. (2016). University teachers' beliefs of language and content integration in English-medium education in multilingual settings. In T. Nikula, E. Dafouz, P. Moore & U. Smit (Eds.), *Conceptualising integration in CLIL and multilingual education* (pp. 123–143). Bristol: Multilingual Matters.

Dafouz, E., & Smit, U. (2016). Towards a dynamic conceptual framework for English-medium education in multilingual university settings. *Applied Linguistics*, *37*(3), 397–415.

Dafouz, E., & Smit, U. (2020). *ROAD-MAPPING English medium education in the internationalised university*. London: Palgrave Macmillan.

Dearden, J., & Macaro, E. (2016). Higher education teachers' attitudes towards English medium instruction: A three-country comparison. *Studies in Second Language Learning and Teaching*, *6*(3), 455–486.

Duarte, J., & Van der Ploeg, M. (2019). Plurilingual lecturers in English medium instruction in the Netherlands: The key to plurilingual approaches in higher education? *European Journal of Higher Education*, *9*(3), 268–284.

García, O. (2009). *Bilingual education in the 21st century: A global perspective*. Malden, MA; Oxford: Wiley-Blackwell.

Hadley, G. (2015). *English for academic purposes in neoliberal universities: A critical grounded theory*. Dordrecht: Springer.

Hellekjaer, G. O. (2006). Screening criteria for English-medium programmes: A case study. In R. Wilkinson, V. Zegers & C. van Leeuwen (Eds.), *Bridging the assessment gap in English-medium higher education* (pp. 43–60). Bochum: AKS–Verlag.

Hu, G., & Lei, J. (2014). English-medium instruction in Chinese higher education: A case study. *Higher Education*, *67*(5), 551–567.

Hyland, K. (2012). *Disciplinary identities*. Cambridge: Cambridge University Press.

Jenkins, J., Cogo, A., & Dewey, M. (2011). Review of developments in research into English as a Lingua Franca. *Language Teaching*, *44*(3), 281–315.

Jiang, L., Zhang, L. J., & May, S. (2019). Implementing English-medium instruction (EMI) in China: Teachers' practices and perceptions, and students' learning motivation and needs. *International Journal of Bilingual Education and Bilingualism*, *22*(2), 107–119.

Krashen, S. (1985). *The Input hypothesis: Issues and implications*. London: Longman.

Lueg, K., & Lueg, R. (2015). Why do students choose English as a medium of instruction? A Bourdieusian perspective on the study strategies of non-native English speakers. *Academy of Management Learning and Education*, *14*(1), 5–30.

Macaro, E. (2018). *English medium instruction*. Oxford: Oxford University Press.

Moncada-Comas, B., & Block, D. (2019). CLILised EMI in practice: Issues arising. *Language Learning Journal*. doi:10.1080/09571736.2019.1660704.

Phillipson, R., & Skutnabb-Kangas, T. (2013). Linguistic imperialism and endangered languages. In T. K. Bhatia & W. C. Ritchie (Eds.), *The handbook of bilingualism and multilingualism* (2nd ed., pp. 495–516). Malden, MA: Wiley-Blackwell.

Piller, I., & Cho, J. (2013). Neoliberalism as language policy. *Language in Society*, *42*(1), 23–44.
Sánchez-Pérez, M. (Ed.). (2020). *Teacher training for English-medium instruction in higher education*. Hershey, PA: IGI Global.
Shohamy, E. (2013). A critical perspective on the use of English as a medium of instruction at universities. In A. Doiz, D. Lasagabaster & J. M. Sierra (Eds.), *English-medium instruction at universities: Global challenges* (pp. 196–213). London: Longman. doi:10.21832/9781847698162-014.
Silver, R. E., & Lwin, S. M. (2013). *Language in education: Social implications*. London: A&C Black.
Söderlundh, H. (2012). Global policies and local norms: Sociolinguistic awareness and language choice at an international university. *International Journal of the Sociology of Language*, *216*, 87–109.
Swain, M., & Lapkin, S. (1995). Problems in output and the cognitive processes they generate: A step towards second language learning. *Applied Linguistics*, *16*(3), 371–391.
Tatzl, D. (2011). English-medium masters' programmes at an Austrian university of applied sciences: Attitudes, experiences and challenges. *Journal of English for Academic Purposes*, *10*(4), 252–270.
Unterberger, B. (2014). *English-medium degree programmes in Austrian tertiary business studies: Policies and programme design* (Doctoral Dissertation). University of Vienna, Austria. Reterived February 15, 2020, from http://othes.univie.ac.at/33961/.
Van der Walt, C., & Kidd, M. (2013). Acknowledging academic biliteracy in higher education assessment strategies: A tale of two trials. In A. Doiz, D. Lasagabaster & J. M. Sierra (Eds.), *English-medium instruction at universities: Global challenges* (pp. 27–43). Bristol: Multilingual Matters.
Werther, C., Denver, L., Jensen, C., & Mees, I. M. (2014). Using English as a medium of instruction at university level in Denmark: The lecturer's perspective. *Journal of Multilingual and Multicultural Development*, *35*(5), 443–462. doi: 10.1080/01434632.2013.868901.
Wilkinson, R. (2013). English-medium instruction at a Dutch University: Challenges and pitfalls. In A. Doiz, D. Lasagabaster & J. M. Sierra (Eds.), *English-medium instruction at universities: Global challenges* (pp. 3–24). Bristol: Multilingual Matters.

Index

Note: Page numbers in **bold** denote tables, in *italic* denote figures.

academic discipline 11, 96, 116, 122
academic discourse 63, 122, 125
academic English 31, 38, 74
academic identity 47, 51, 59–63, 65, 67, 73, 80
academic language 22, 35, 38
academic literacies 116
Ackerley, K. 20, 35, 37, 125
Ackerley, K. *et al.* 21
agents 11, 14, 27, 36, 61–2, 70–6, 78, 89–91, 98, 123 *see also* educational agents
Aguilar, M and Arnó, E. 13, 19, 25, 28, 32
Aguilar, M and Rodriguez, R. 122
Aguilar, M. 19, 21, 35, 96
Airey, J. 14, 20, 21, 28, 29, 37, 38, 96, 127
Airey, J. and Linder, C. 65
Alderson, C. and Wall, D. 99
Andrade, H.G. 99
Arkin, E. and Osam, N. 4
Armengol, L. *et al.* 71
Arnó, E. and Aguilar, M. 32
Arnó, E. *et al.* 38
Arnó-Macià, E. and Mancho Barés, G. 21
ASSEMID 1, 4, 13, 19, 78, 82, 100, 108, 121
assessment 1, 5, 7, 77, 80, 82, 97–9, 104, 111, 114–16, 122, 128 *see also* evaluation
audio log 4, 71, 81–2, 89

backstage 13, 43–9, 51, 59–61, 63–6, 74–5, 86–7, 124–5

Baker, W. and Hüttner, J. 9, 96, 127
Ball, P. and Lindsay, D. 20, 98, 114
Barnard, R. and Hasim, Z. 1
Başıbek, N. *et al.* 122
Basturkmen, H. 96, 127
being a student 13, 43, 46–50, 60–2, 64, 65, 73–4, 76, 91, 125
Benwell, B.M. and Stokoe, E.M. 13, 44, 46–7, 60, 64–5, 73, 76
bilingual 8, 22, 31, 48, 49, 71, 89, 101, 103, 121, 122
bilingualism 19
Blackledge, A. and Creese, A. 50
Block, D. 50, 70, 102, 121
Block, D. and Moncada-Comas, B. 96, 102, 125, 127
Blommaert, J. 11
Borràs, E. and Moore, E. 65
Bourdieu P. 121, 122, 124
Bradford, A. 21
Bradford, A. and Brown, H. 1
Breeze, R. and Dafouz, E. 98, 99, 116
Breeze, R. and Sancho-Guinda, C. 1, 2
Brenn-White, M. and Faethe, E. 1
Bretxa, V. *et al.* 1
Brown, P. and Levinson, S.C. 62
Bruton, A. 121
Burns, T. 44–5, 47

Catalan 1–3, 12–14, 19, 21–4, 26–7, 29–33, 35, 48–9, 66, 70–1, 78–82, 84, 86–7, 89, 99–103, 108, 120–4, 126
Catalonia 2–4, 12, 70, 89, 128
certificate 81

134 Index

certification 123
Clark, C. 20
CLIL (Content and Language Integrated Learning) 28, 80–1, 121–2
CLIL-*ised* EMI 21, 28, 38
coding 24, 94
Codó, E. 72, 124
Collini, S. 6
communication 20–2, 27, 34, 37, 38, 61, 72–3, 76, 80, 84, 86–7, 98–9, 101, 104, 106, 108–9, 114–15, 120–1, 125, 128
confirmation check 59
Costa F. and Coleman, J. 3
Costa, F. 96
Costa, F. and Mariotti, C. 4
Cots, J.M. 71
Cowan, K. 50, 63
Crawford Camiciottoli, B. and Campoy-Cubillo, M.C. 50
Cummins, J. 121
curriculum 4, 8, 11, 70, 77, 99

Dafouz, E. 3, 9
Dafouz, E. and Camacho-Miñano, M. 21, 26
Dafouz, E. and Smit, U. 1, 10–11, 128
Dafouz, E., Camacho-Miñano, M. and Urquía-Grande, E. 36
Dafouz, E., Hüttner, J. and Smit, U. 96, 127
Dafouz-Milne, E. 71
Dardot, P. and Laval, C. 6
Davies, B. and Harré, R. 47, 100
Dearden, J. 8
Dearden, J., and Macaro, E. 27, 36, 38, 123
Dimova, S. and Kling, J. 20, 21, 30, 34, 98
Dimova, S. *et al.* 1, 27
disciplinary complexity 121, 125–6
disciplinary knowledge 21–2, 32, 36, 44, 65–6, 77–8, 81, 88, 99, 108, 110, 114, 126, 128
disciplinary literacies 21, 28, 37–8
discourse 9–11, 21, 28, 43, 48, 63, 96, 99, 104, 110, 114–15, 122, 125–8
doing education 13, 43–4, 46–8, 50–1, 59–64, 66–7, 73–4, 76, 82, 84, 86, 89, 91, 125

Doiz, A. and Lasagabaster, D. 2
Doiz, A., Lasagabaster, D. and Sierra, J.M. 2
Doiz, A., Costa, F., Lasagabaster, D. and Mariotti, C. 21, 25, 26, 35
domain loss 7, 8
Duarte, J. and Van der Ploeg, M. 124
Duchêne, A. *et al.* 71

EAP (English for Academic Purposes) 1, 8, 28, 37
educational agents 70–6, 90–1
educational 4, 8, 70–6, 90–1, 98, 115
Egron-Polak, E. 6
EHEA (European Higher Education Area) 9, 12
ELF (English as a lingua franca) 8–10
elitism 123–4
elitist 122
Elliott, N. *et al.* 2
EME (English-Medium Education) 5, 8, 10, 11
EMEMUS (English Medium Education in Multilingual University Settings) 11, 128
EMI (English-Medium Instruction) in Higher Education (HE) 2–4, 14
EMI at Universitat de Lleida and Universitat Politècnica de Catalunya 12
EMI implementation 19, 24, 26–7, 35–6, 38, 90, 123–4
EMI in STEM 1
EMI lecturer 20, 22, 24, 38, 43, 71–4, 76, 89, 96–8, 101, 116, 120–1, 123–4, 127–8
EMI policy 70
EMI programme 9–10, 20
EMI student 21, 25–6, 31–33, 35–6, 43, 60, 66, 73–4, 89
EMI, role of language in 30
English language 3, 8, **25**, 37, 71–4, 78
English, low use of 126
Englishisation 5, 7–8, 48, 70–2, 74, 89–90, 124
Ennew, C. and Greenaway, D. 5
equality of learning opportunities 121
ESP (English for Specific Purposes) 1, 8, 19–20, 23–6, 28, 29, 34, 37–8, 120
European 3, 4, 9, 71, 121

evaluation 4, 23, 33, 64, 96–7, 99, 104, 106, 108–9, 11, 113–14, 121
exam 4, 20, 23, 34, 46, 78, 79, 82, **83**, 84–6, 108, 124

Fairclough, N. 5
feedback 14, 64, 83, 87–8, 96–7, 99, 102, 113–15, 121, 128
Fenton-Smith, B. *et al.* 1
Ferguson, G. 8
field notes 4
Firth, A. 76
Flores, N. 6
Flubacher, M. *et al.* 72
fluency 20, 35, 37, 81, **106**, 107, 111, 114, 127
Fortanet-Gómez, I. 1, 2, 4
Foucault, M. 96
frontstage 13, 43–9, 51, 60, 63, 74–5, 82, 86–8, 91, 124–5

García, O. 124
gaze 43, 50–1, 125
gesture 43, 46–7, 51, 60–2, 64, 125
Gierlinger, E.M. 4
Giroux, H. 72, 90
global 7, 9, 70–2, 74, 121
globalization 11
Goffman, E. 13, 44, 45, 47, 51, 59, 60, 62, 74
Guarda, M. 20, 26
Guarda, M. and Helm, F. 20, 21, 27

Haberland, H. 8
Haberland, H. and Mortensen, J. 2
Hadley, G. 124
Hazel, S. and Mortensen, J. 71, 75
Hellekjær, G.O. 21, 26–8
Hellekjær, G.O. and Wilkinson, R. 29
Heller, M. 13
Henrikson, B. *et al.* 1
higher education 4–5, 9, 11, 66, 96, 98
Hultgren, A.K. 8
Hultgren, A.K. *et al.* 1, 5
Hyland, K. 11, 96, 100, 127
Hyland, K. and Shaw, P.H. 2

identity 21, 46–7, 49–51, 59–65, 67, 72–3, 76, 86, 125
immersion 27, 33, 37, 126

institutional policy 20, 24, 27, 120, 123
instruction 10; language of 13, 19–20, 26, 31, 33, 36, 88, 122:
English-only 13
interaction 13, 27, 43, 45–50, 59–60, 62–6, 71, 74–6, 78, 82, 86–90, 96, 100, 103, 122, 125, 127
interactional episodes 43, 46, 50
international 3, 6–12
internationalisation 5–7, 9–12
interview 3–4, 13, 22–3, 24, 26, 29, 31, 36, 78, 80, 82, 86, 101, 103, 107–10, 114, 124

Jenkins, J. 2
Jenkins, J. and Mauranen, A. 2
Jenkins, J. *et al.* 125
Jewit, C. *et al.* 50
Jiang, L. *et al.* 20, 37, 125
Johnson, K.E. and Golombek, P.R. 24, 29
Jonsson, A. and Svingby, G. 98

Kim, E.G. *et al.* 33, 37
Krashen. S. 127
Kubota, R. 6
Kuteeva, M. 2

L1 8, 19–26, 28–39, 43, 46, 66–7, 81, 103, 120, 124, 126–8
L1 mediated instruction 3
L1 mediated undergraduate programmes 13
L1 medium instruction 13, 66
L2 66, 127
language improvement 33, 37
language in education policies 71
language in education: 70–2, 90–1, 121, 127
language learning 27, 28, 33, 35, 38, 67, 81, 97, 100, 106, 115
language of instruction 13, 19–20, 26, 31, 33, 36, 38, 88, 122
language teaching 78, 96, 100, 106–7, 109–11, 114–5
Lasagabaster, D. and Ruiz de Zarobe, Y. 2
Lasagabaster, D. *et al.* 73
Law, D. and Hoey, M. 5
Lea, M.R. and Street, B.V. 116

Index

lecturer self-selection *see* self-selection
Lei, J. and Hu. G. 21
Li, Ch. and Ruan, Z. 21
local language 70–4, 80, 82, 84–6, 88–91, 120, 123–4, 126
Lueg, K. and Lueg, R. 121–2

Macaro, E. 121
Macaro, E. *et al.* 20
MacCannell, D. 46
Mancho-Barés, G. and Aguilar-Perez, M. 102
Mancho-Barés, G. and Arnó-Macià, E. 71, 80
Manning, P. 44, 62
marketisation 5–6
Martín Rojo, L. 70, 73–4
material 32, 35–6, 49–50
McCormack, C. 24
methodology 3, 24, 28, 43, 49, 67, 77, 101, **109**
Meyrowitz, J. 44–6
microphenomena 4, 71, 120, 128
mode 50–1, 59, 63
Moncada-Comas, B. and Block, D. 35, 38, 73, 96, 127
Mondada, L. 49–50
Moore, E. *et al.* 72, 76, 86
Morell, T. 43, 50, 66
Mortensen, J. 70, 74
Mortensen, J. and Haberland, H. 70
Mukerji, S. and Tripathi, P. 2
multilingualism 8, 10–11, 70–2, 74, 76, 78, 89–91, 122–3, 128
multimodal 43–44, 49–51, 60, 63–6, 82, 90, 100, 120–1, 125–8
Murata, K. *et al.* 2

neoliberal 5–6, 70, 72–4, 90, 121–2, 124, 128
Nikula, T. *et al.* 2
Nilsson, B. 9
Norris, S. 43, 50–1

oral presentation 14, 82–3, 96–7, 99, 102–4, 108–9, 111, 115–6, 127

Panadero, E. and Jonnson, A. 98
Pecorari D. and Malmström, H. 2
Pecorari, D. *et al.* 20, 34

peer 61–3, 66, 106, 116
peer-scaffolding 51, *55*, 59–63, 65–7
peer-to-peer 78, 82, 86–7, 124–5, 127
Pennycook, A. 7
Phillipson, R. 7
Phillipson, R. and Skutnabb-Kangas, T. 121
Piller, I. and Cho, J. 70, 121, 124
plurilingual 72, 74, 80, 82, 84, 91, 120, 124–7
plurilingualism 124–7
policy 1, 2, 4, 27, 30, 36, 39n, 70, 73, 82, 91, 122–3
positioning 47–8, 63, 65–6, 73, 90, 100, 108
PowerPoint 35, 76–7, 79, 84, 91n4, 99, 101, 112, 117n5
Preisler, B. 76
Preisler, B. *et al.* 2
presentation *see* oral presentation
Prieto Martín, A. *et al.* 77
proficiency 3, 20–1, 26–8, 29, 35–8, 48, 77, 79, 81–2, 90–1, 97–8, 114, 121–2, 126, 128

question 22–4, 37, 43, 49, 51, *57*, 59–60, 63–67, 72, 78, 81–3, 85–90, 97, 99, 101–3, **106**, 108–9, 111, 114, **119**, 121, 125, 127
questionnaire 3, 4, 13, 79, 81–2, 121

recording *see* video
Reddy, Y.M. and Andrade, H. 97–8
resistance 47, 71–6, 82, 86–7, 89–91, 124 *see also* whispers of resistance
Ribeiro, B.T. 47–8
ROADMAPPING framework 11, 124
Robinson, L. and Schulz, J. 45
Rose, H. *et al.* 37
Rose, H. *et al.* 75
Roth, W. 61
rubric 4, 14, 78, 96–100, 104, 106, 108, 109, 111–7, 121, 128
Ruiz de Zarobe, Y. *et al.* 2

Saldaña, J. 24
Sánchez-Pérez, M. 123
scaffolding 28–9, 35, 37–8, 51, 55, 59–61, 63, 65–7, 122
Schegloff, E. and Sacks, H. 83

self-positioning 14
self-selection 25–7, 36, 38, 121–3
Shohamy, E. 121, 123
Silver, R.E. and Lwin, S.M. 127
Simbolon, N.E. 4
skills 20–1, 28, 31–2, 35, 37–8, 77, 79, 82, 97–8, 104–5, 111, 114, 116, 126–7
Smit, U. 4, 45
Smit, U. and Dafouz, E. 2
Smit, U. and Studer, P. 2
Smyth, J. 6
sociolinguistics 11, 13, 71, 89, 120, 122, 124
socio-political 71–2
Söderlundh, H. 70, 71, 74–6, 83, 124
Spanish 1, 3, **12**, 14, 19, 21, 22, 30–1, 48–9, 67, 71, 79–82, 84–5, 88, 90, 92, 94, 99, 101–3, **116**, 122–4, 126
Spolsky, B. 73
stakeholders 2, 4, 11, 22, 90, 121, 124
see also educational agents
STEM (Science Technology Engineering and Mathematics) 1, 7, 14, 97, 100, 121, 128
Stevens, D. and Levi, A.J. 97
Sunal, D.W., *et al.* 116
survey 3, 22–6, 31, 36–7, 124 *see also* questionnaire
Swain, M. and Lapkin, S. 127

Tadic, N. 64
task 30, 46–7, 49, 59, 64–5, 73–5, 77, 82–4, 85–8, 91, 98, 101, 124–5, 128
Tatzl, D. 21, 37, 122
teaching methodology 101
technical vocabulary 35–6, 96

terminology 20–1, 37, 80, 85–6, 89, 102, 110
Thompson, G. *et al.* 37
Thornborrow, J. and Haarman, L. 44
translation 30, **67**, 80, 82, 85, 87–8, 95
trilingual 3
trilingualism 30
Tsou, W. and Kao, Sh–M. 20

UCLES (University of Cambridge Local Examinations Syndicate) 79
UdL (Universitat de Lleida) 1, 5, 7, 10, 12, 14, 79, 89, 124
Unterberger, B. 27, 38, 123
UPC (Universitat Politècnica de Catalunya) 1, 5, 10, 12–13, 19, 35
Urciuoli, B. 6

Valcke, J. and Wilkinson, R. 2, 4
Van der Walt, C. 2
Van der Walt, C. and Kidd, M. 122
video 3, 13, 30, 35, 49, 51, 63, 67, **88**, 90, **109**
Vygotsky, L.S. 61

Wachter, B. and Maiworm, F. 2
Werther, C. *et al.* 122–3
whispers of resistance 14, 71–4, 76, 82, 84, 86, 90, 124
Wiggins, G. 98
Wilkinson, R. 96, 121
Williams, J. 6
Wood, D. *et al.* 61

Zhang, Z. and Chan, E. 21, 28, 38
Zhao, J. and Dixon, L. Q. 2

For Product Safety Concerns and Information please contact our EU representative GPSR@taylorandfrancis.com
Taylor & Francis Verlag GmbH, Kaufingerstraße 24, 80331 München, Germany